The Translator: KO WON
Ko Won has published five volumes of his own poetry, all in Korean, and many translations of poetry from Korean into English and from English into Korean. He won the 1966 Kansas City Star poetry contest for poems written in English.

"When Ko Won writes in a poem, 'the lamplight grows under my skin/still facing midnight,' he speaks as a man who knows midnight as well as a child knows his own room. He experienced war in both North and South Korea. As poet and as person he has a shrewd sense of Korean verse from the past decades, of the luck and pain out of which it was written."— Paul Engle

CONTEMPORARY
KOREAN
POETRY

IOWA
TRANSLATIONS

PAUL ENGLE

GENERAL EDITOR

CONTEMPORARY KOREAN POETRY

COMPILED AND TRANSLATED BY

KO WON

UNIVERSITY OF IOWA PRESS Ψ IOWA CITY

Library of Congress Catalog Card Number: 74-113487
University of Iowa Press, Iowa City 52240
© 1970 by The University of Iowa. All rights reserved
Printed in the United States of America
Designed by John B. Goetz

ISBN 87745-002-1

Foreword

Theology once believed that "translation" could mean direct removal of the body to heaven without intervening death. All too often in being translated, the poem loses its life.

Literal translation of a poem into bare prose may help understanding, but the plain text of a literal version may not be accurate to the poem, for what a poet writes is not a literal account of his life, but an imaginative vision of it. Only a translator with imagination can truly translate the imaginative language of a poem.

The Iowa Translations series brings together people of creative talent with those expert in a language. We believe that in the hazardous twentieth century men of good mind and good will must talk to each other or die. We believe that poetry is the highest form of talk, and that translating it is therefore an honor and a privilege as well as one of the toughest jobs known to man.

When Ko Won writes in a poem, "the lamplight grows under my skin/still facing midnight," he speaks as a man who knows midnight as well as a child knows his own room. He experienced war in both North and South Korea. As poet and as person he has a shrewd sense of Korean verse from the past decades, of the luck and pain out of which it was written. He also has a fine feeling toward the shape of a poem in English. Yi Chang-hŭi wrote that he felt green spring in a cat's whiskers. We feel it also in these poems.

PAUL ENGLE, General Editor
Director, International Writing Program
School of Letters, The University of Iowa

The Translator

Ko Won, pseudonym of Ko Sŏng-wŏn, was born in Korea and graduated from Tongguk University. He studied English at Queen Mary College, University of London, and creative writing at The University of Iowa, where he received an M.F.A. in English. He is presently a doctoral candidate in comparative literature at New York University. He was formerly Secretary of the Korean Center for the International P.E.N., while teaching college in Seoul, and has traveled widely. He has published five volumes of poetry, *Antinomic Contradiction* (1954), *The Love Song of the Sun* (1956), *At the Time Appointed with Eyes* (1960), *Far Is Today* (1963), and *The Whispering Fire's Flower* (1964), all in Korean, and many translations of poetry both from Korean into English and from English into Korean, including D. H. Lawrence's *Look! We Have Come Through!* He writes poetry in English too, and won the *Kansas City Star* Award in poetry for 1966.

Preface

Some of Ko Won's work, in preparing this anthology of Korean po-
etry, was done while he was participating in and assisting The Univer-
sity of Iowa Translation Workshop. His own commitment, loyalty,
and labor brought the anthology to flower; but some of the seeds
were planted in the Translation Workshop.

The idea of such a workshop was first made reality by Paul Engle
in 1963; since that time much good work has been done inside the
workshop's invisible walls. This Workshop lies in a beautiful no
man's land between The University of Iowa's academic English De-
partment and its creative Writers Workshop; on that land it fights
battles all its own. The ideal of those battles is noble; to bring home
living texts, living prisoners, after having overcome them with the
weapons both of creation and scholarship. The reality has often
conformed to some version of this ideal, failing most often in regard
to the word "living."

For this failure there are several possible reasons: the incompe-
tence of the translator or the translated; the timidity of the transla-
tor; and, astonishingly seldom, the intractability of the text to be
translated. Ko Won's careful daring has helped him to sidestep all
these failures. He is a poet with nerve translating poets with nerve.
Above all, he is aware of the suppleness of language. This awareness
expresses itself here, and makes a fresh work. It is part of his nerve.

I refer to the instinct by which Ko Won hews to an implicit theory
about the translation of poetry; that such remaking should do some
violence to the language into which the translation is made. This
theory is not popular. Most translations of poetry, even of modern
poetry, attempt to offer a tamed version. At their most risking they

try to be not only faithful but good, right up to the level of their originals. This effort is, properly, the leitmotif of translators of prose fiction. Translators of novels, at least of novels in any relation to the realist tradition, must bring over into the new language dialogue which is readable and natural; and they must represent a named surrounding world which is directly intelligible to the reader. However this is not — and shouldn't be — the burden of the translator of poetry. Ko Won wisely goes much less far than this in bringing twentieth-century Korean poetry to us. He makes us go some distance toward it.

He worries us very nicely. He refuses not to make us work for the new perceptions which quite naturally find themselves in a literature as far from ours as Korean. He faces us with a "white, dreamy field"; a soul cries "free my love back to me"; the Russian motto V NAROD is thrust into English; "the far hills coldly strike" the poet's "brow"; a cloud "circles around/the clean eyes/of a green deer." None of this quite strikes the tone of colloquial English, none of it is correct in the tiresome sense; and all of it pulls us out a little farther toward the boundaries of our sense for our "own language." Perhaps this last phrase is the most important.

One thing Ko Won helps us to understand, through these translations, is an important sense in which "our" language is not our own. (I pass over the substance, Korean poetry, through which he helps this understanding.) We simply don't possess English. No one does. No one can. We can lay out stakes of usage, but those can easily be pulled up and placed back farther from the center. Ko Won has a tendency to do this. If all languages are continually enlarged in this way, do their borders tend to unite? Do we grow closer to that oneness of language mentioned, by Ko Won in his Introduction, as one of the goals of the Korea Proletariat Artist Federation in 1925?

FREDERIC WILL
Director, Translation Workshop
The University of Iowa

• x •

ACKNOWLEDGMENTS

Grateful acknowledgment is given to the following publishers for permission to reprint the poems in this book:

The Asia Foundation, San Francisco: *The Asian Student*, March 27, 1965, for "The Words of a Certain Poet" by Kim Su-yŏng, and "Flower" by Kim Ch'un-su.

Micromegas, Iowa City: *Micromegas*, I–1, 1965, for "Esquisse" by Cho Hyang.

Verb Publications, Denver: *Metaphrasis* (1965) for "An Episode" by Cho Hyang, "Resistance in June" by Kim Chong-mun, "Flower" by Kim Ch'un-su, "Life" by Sin Tong-jip, "The Last Conversation" by Pak In-hwan, "Flag of Mind" by Kim Nam-jo, and "Shooting at the Moon" by Kim Yo-sŏp.

Doshisha University Press, Kyoto, Japan: *The East-West Review*, II–3, 1966, for "Fade to Enter" by Chŏng Han-mo, and "Fallen Leaves Live Together" by Cho Pyŏng-hwa.

Introduction

This anthology of twentieth-century Korean poetry contains 184 poems written by 141 poets ranging from the first through the present decade, and they are divided into two parts. Section I may give the reader a bird's-eye view of the development of modern Korean poetry until, roughly, the end of World War II, when Korea was liberated from Japanese rule. In Section II, where the order is chronological by author, I have put the poets whose works translated here were written after the liberation, although some of the authors started publishing earlier. Since translatability was one of the primary considerations in my selection, these poets are not necessarily always represented by what are commonly considered their "best" works. Many younger poets, I am afraid, more than the older, have been left out in the selection, partly because I did not have their poems that fit translation at this time and partly because of space. In South Korea alone, there are now well over three hundred "published poets," and it was neither possible nor desirable for me to present them all.

Furthermore, I have excluded the Communist poets in the North because, despite their sharing a common language, the culture and therefore the poetry of North Korea in its Communist phase, that is, since 1945, is virtually alien. North Korean poetry would probably be best suited for a separate book. On the other hand, I have given some examples of the *sijo*, the traditional form of Korean poetry, which had begun to develop in the late Koryŏ Dynasty (918–1392) and was most popular during the Yi Dynasty (1392–1910). The writing of *sijo* poetry on various subjects was overwhelmingly stimulated by the invention of a purely Korean alphabet, the *hangŭl*, in

1443. Apart from the matter of its recitation, the basic form of written *sijo* is a three-line stanza: two phrases in each line — making six altogether; four feet per line, three to five syllables in a foot, with the variation of 42 to 46 syllables in totality. The pattern is thus something like this: first line — 3,4/3(4),4; second — 3,4/3(4),4; and third — 3,5/4,3. Although it is now customary to separate the tradition from *poetry*, I thought it would be appropriate for this book to include those contemporary writers who are particularly interested in the *sijo*.

Korean personal names are put in the Korean manner with the family name coming first: for instance, Chu Yo-han instead of Yo-han Chu. When a pseudonym is used, it is not hyphenated. The dates of composition and publication, where available, are provided in Section I at the end of each poem: the former on the left side of the page and the latter on the right.

In the beginning of this century, shortly before Korea was forced to accept the so-called "annexation" to Japan in 1910, a turning point in the history of Korean literature had been marked by the "new literature" movement. It drew a clear line between the old literary tradition and the application of Western style and method to the writing of modern Korean literature. The "new poetry" worked obviously toward a viable vernacular Korean prosody and was identified with free verse and the use of more familiar idiom.

This was first exemplified by a prominent historian Ch'oe Namsŏn (1890–1957) who published his famous poem *From the Sea to Children* in 1908. Here are two stanzas from it.

1

Splash, splash, slap, and roll.
The sea lashes, smashes, crushes.
Great mountains, stately rocks,
all is nothing, nothing at all.
"My power, know it or not?", roaring so,
the sea lashes, smashes, crushes.
Splash, splash, rumble, and boom.

6

Splash, splash, slap, and roll.
I hate the world and people on the whole,
but one thing I love above all:

that is children, brave and innocent,
coming and nestling in my bosom, so lovely.
Come, children, I will kiss you.
Splash, splash, rumble, and boom.

The poem, which has many onomatopoetic lines, can hardly be said to be great, but the whole tone was quite revolutionary to Korean ears, and it sounded a new note, namely the power of youth and the importance of a new generation. The date of its publication was so significant that the history of modern Korean poetry is usually counted from this year.

The year 1919 was another important date: the nation-wide Independence Movement flared up with little success; an epoch was marked in bringing in what is called the "Korean Renaissance." The establishment of not a few literary magazines, beginning with the *Ch'angjo* (*Creation*, 1919–21), all short-lived, yet quite active, made a great contribution to a pure literature, intended to counteract the previous attempt to bring about enlightenment and social reform. It was in 1919 that an important prose poem by Chu Yo-han, *Playing with Fire*, was published. Strictly speaking, the first "new poetry" was demonstrated by the symbolistic expressions of Chu and some of his contemporaries. For this reason, I have chosen to let him lead off this book. The following is an excerpt from his poem, chosen for its exemplary and historical rather than its literary qualities.

Oh it dances, glowing red a fire-ball dances, as seen from the top of a quiet castle-gate, the smell of water and of sand is biting the night and the sky, and a torch biting itself off, ...
. . . .
Oh the river laughs, laughs, that's a funny laugh, laughter of the cold water laughing at the dark water. Oh a boat is coming up, a boat rises, sadly, sadly creaking with every gust of wind.
. . . .
Oh burn it, burn it up tonight, you — the red torch, your eyes, and your red tears.

The failure of the "March 1 Movement" for independence in 1919 brought about a predominant trend of pessimism and dejection throughout the country. In literature, however, it gave rise to the period (1920–30) which the critic Pak Yŏng-hŭi (1901–?) called "a golden age of poetry in the world of Korean literature." It was characterized by the superimposing of the techniques of European and American romanticism, symbolism, decadence, and aestheticism upon Korean attitudes and themes. A good many of these Korean romantic poets shared a sentimental, lyrical, idealistic, and nationalistic nature. No technical term seems appropriate enough to cover the whole of this trend, and yet there was something specifically Korean, which I will try to explain briefly in the following paragraphs.

It may be helpful to the reader for understanding especially those poems in Section I of this book if he comes to notice that most of the symbols the poets frequently use very closely express the political and social situations of Korea under Japanese control. It is interesting, perhaps natural too, that although Korean and Western literature chooses its symbols from a common fund, differences in emphasis persist. For example, sunset, evening, night, and autumn as well as darkness and falling leaves must necessarily connote time in any culture. But the preference of these symbols over their opposites, which of course also connote time, was characteristic of the Korean pessimism of that difficult historical moment. In other words, the Korean romanticists and symbolists of this period could not be happy as Robert Browning was in singing: "The Year's at the Spring/And day's at the morn;/Morning's at seven;/ . . . All's right with the world." While their soil was not their own, they cared only for some future spring. Yi Sang-hwa cries out "Does spring come even to the plundered field?" (1926). They felt more themselves contemplating falling flowers. And they found themselves wandering about in autumn, weeping with Verlaine: "Et je m'en vais/Au vent mauvais/Qui m'emporte/Deçà, delà,/Pareil à la/ Feuille morte."

The philosophy of transience and nothingness is of course not at all new to Korea, but in this period it was expressed with great bleakness, for now with their land taken from them, Koreans deeply felt the despair of the loss of their cultural heritage. At the same time, the new generation of poets was able to draw on its own traditional notions of mutability and eternal recurrence. The regenerative aspect of the notion of transience, the notion of simple endurance, always implicit in these Eastern conceptions, became increasingly apparent, so that the very symbols of death and dying in Korean poetry mirrored forth their opposite.

Night, thus, is something special. Day is gone, it is dark, and the country is dark, so is the mind of the people, and the night goes on and on. The picture of darkness, however, is a little more complicated than that. This is the time for Koreans to escape an obvious situation in which they are under pressure, desperately depressed, to sit and think or talk freely with those who have interests in common, and to dream of something better. The dream, as in European Symbolism, is favored in Korean poetry. It is interesting to note: night in Western poetry *usually* implies death, but it is not always so in Korean poetry. On the contrary, it may well imply birth and life, that is also a dream, in connection with the lost country. Chu Yo-han, for instance, prays at night as a child to go out to meet "Him," not necessarily Christ only but a supernatural power, and to "talk to Him about you," you or mother here possibly meaning Korea.

> After you have put me in bed at ease,
> I will slip out to meet Him there
> in the white, dreamy field,
> and will talk to Him about you.

The interpretation of night made by O Sang-sun, a nihilistic life-time wanderer, may interest the reader. He once pronounced in his poem, *The Last Night-scene of Asia* (1922), that "truth of Asia is that of night." Although this is much broader than a Korean "scene," Asia must have meant to him the continent to which the darkened Korea belonged. The night to him was "the symbol of Asian mind," the "mother and midwife," "master and god," "heart, eye, ear, senses, reason, sexual desire, appetite, drinks, religion, the only love and pride and treasure and glory, palace of soul . . . of Asia."

There often comes rain, which is tears and a force that causes leaves and flowers and grain to fall down. Like Verlaine, again, Korean poets weep, "Il pleure dans mon coeur/Comme il pleut sur la ville," but their answer to the question, "Quelle est cette langueur/Qui pénètre mon coeur?" is clear. At about the time when T. S. Eliot wrote *The Wasteland*, Korean poets were lamenting the desolateness of the more specific ruined land, which was the image of the Korean mind. Not only negative, however, the rain is also symbolized as a source of life. In fact, it has much to do with farming in Korea.

Snow, again, does not imply death as often as in Western poetry.

Instead, snow makes people feel warm, protects barley and grass from death in winter. Its color is very important. The whiteness is almost always directly associated with the white color of the most common Korean clothes. The whiteness being the color of innocence functions metaphorically as well. So it goes with white cloud, white egret, white sea gull, white road, white flower, and white mind, etc. Incidentally, an important literary magazine published in 1922 through 1923 was called the *Paekcho*, meaning the "white tide," and its Korean sound is exactly the same as that of swan, which is significant especially in Western Symbolist poetry.

The ideas of flight, flowing, parting, and departure can be interpreted as the psychology of Koreans during this particular period. Almost all the Korean writers, their sense of value limiting them to the past and somewhere outside the world, had the strong tendency of escapism and resignation. Contemplating the real world, a poet laments that he is a "breathing mummy" (Kim Hyŏng-wŏn), and another poet declares himself "a king of tears" (Hong Sa-yong). In a situation in which they find little hope, the poets wish to stay away from home without knowing where to go, and they frequently use the images of bird, cloud, and boat to express this desperation. Their departure *for somewhere* is often forced:

> One who has to leave, being driven, and people
> he leaves behind, all will be long remembered.
> The wind plays with the clouds as I look back.
> No place prepared ahead for my entrance.
> > Pak Yong-ch'ŏl, *Departing Boat*

Sometimes, more often than not, even the biblical reference prompts the national tragedy. "Madonna" in Yi Sang-hwa's *To My Bedroom* (composed in 1918), is a beautifully spiritualized and idealized woman standing for the lost country. The poet feels an urgent need for his love, Madonna here, and calls to her in such a sensual and personal tone.

> *Madonna,* I am waiting for you trembling with fears
> in the dark nooks of my mind.
> O the first cock crows already, and all dogs are barking.
> My love, do you hear too?

Madonna, let us go to my bedroom, to the bedroom I made
ready all last night.
. . . .
Madonna, sooner or later we must go. Why don't we go,
then, of our free will, not dragged?
You are my *Maria* who believes in my word, who knows
my bedroom as a cave of resurrection.

"Nim" or "im," the Korean word for "the beloved," when used
in early poems, nearly always means the country. For example,
a poem by Hwang Sŏg-u, *Handing Love Over*, shows the use of both
love and the biblical source in this way.

Look, my soul is blood-dark like the sky
where flashes the death's lightning.
Lying flat as when Christ prayed at Gethsemane,
listen, it cries, "Free my love back to me."

All this, however, is not to say that every Korean poet of the early
modern period wrote nationalistic poetry exclusively, but rather is
to emphasize that Korean poetry becomes more comprehensible
with this sort of background held in mind. Compare one aspect of
Irish literature.

In the case of Han Yong-un, a Buddhist monk and a highly meta-
physical poet again in the Korean sense, "nim" is far more compli-
cated than a national implication. The notion of "the beloved,"
"you," and "love" is a keypoint to understanding his poetry. Here is
the poet's own explanation which appeared in the preface to his
book of poetry, the *Nim ŭi Ch'immuk* (*The Silence of My Love*,
1926.)

My beloved is not only my beloved, but everything I long for.
If mankind is the beloved of the Buddha, then philosophy is that
of Kant. If the spring rain is the beloved of the rose, then Italy
is that of Mazzini. My beloved is not only what I love, but also
what loves me.
If love is freedom, then the beloved too is free. But, does the
freedom's good name free you from all the restraints of devo-

tion? Do you have a beloved? If so, it is not the beloved, but your own shadow.

I have been writing these poems longing for a wandering little lamb that has lost its way home in the sunset plain.

A "secret" of this philosophy can be seen in the following lines from the title poem:

> As we fear to part when we meet, so we believe in our
> next meeting when we part.
> Though my beloved is gone, I have not sent her off.
> The song of love, which cannot bear its own tune,
> circles around the silence of my love.

Paradox here is as obviously provocative as in another poem, "Obeying," which is included in this collection. As a matter of fact, the most delicate paradox is often involved in his poetry. The paradoxical view of the Korean poets in general may well be one of the characteristics of their poetry. Kim Sowŏl, a popular poet who wrote in a folk-lyric style, for example, expressed a somewhat similar view in *Azaleas*:

> When you leave, tired of me,
> I will be ready to let you go,
> no complaints, whatsoever.
>
> And I will carpet your way
> with azaleas, armfuls,
> . . . .

From here we move to another area of prewar poetry. While some people were sick of the writers' pessimism and powerlessness, the socialistic thought and movement in Europe enthusiastically influenced the Korean intelligentsia in the 1920s. In literature, thus, the *Sin Kyŏnghyang P'a* ("new tendency school"), connoting an antibourgeois attitude, was formed, and it later developed to the proletarian literature movement, which also meant to support the independence of Korea. "Literature should start from a protest against fatality, and against actuality," said Kim P'albong, who was leading the group. He criticized the Korean intellectual's spiritual enervation in his poem, *Lamentation of the White Hands*, published in the *Kaebyŏk (Beginning of the World*, 1920–26), an influential quasi-literary monthly, in 1924:

> Only in a saying: "V NAROD!" . . .
> proud of the white arms, the useless
> lamentation of the young Russians
> of sixty years past is still with us.
> Café-chair-revolutionists,
> your hands are too white.

Besides such references as "lamentation" and "white," the quoted Russian word, *V NAROD*, meaning "into the people," is significant here, because the "V NAROD Movement," which had originated from late nineteenth-century Russia, was initiated in Korea by two newspapers later in the thirties, and some writers participated in this. We can note that the members of the "New Tendency School" had connection with the socialistic political agents of the time; specifically in a poem called *Before Dawn* (1926) by Pak Par-yang (b. 1905), who is now writing in North Korea.

> Here you are at last.
> I sat up all the long night waiting for you.
> How many times I went out of the village to see
>   you coming,
> while the crows and magpies were singing of the
>   morning!

Even though they produced very few works of good quality, it can be credited to the school that all its writers became alert to the new "tide" of the age. There soon appeared the proletarian literature when the Korea Proletariat Artist Federation was organized in the summer of 1925. This was usually called "KAPF," reading as *kap*, an abbreviation of the Esperanto form of the name, Korea Artista Proleta Federacio. It is interesting that those involved at the time, both in Japan and Korea, were particularly fond of Esperanto, probably because they wanted to link the Communist idea with an international language. Characteristically, the criticism and arguments among writers and critics between 1925 and 1930 were very active for the first time in the history of Korean literature. In practice, as a whole, the proletarian theory of teleological consciousness and class literature surpassed the production of the artistic quality of works. Let us see some samples of the KAPF members' poetry. The following is an extract from *Wild Swallows* by Pak Se-yŏng (b. 1902), who later wrote the North Korean national anthem.

> You look like the incarnation of liberty.
> Who dare ever seize your bodies?
> . . . .
> Land is cracked like the back of a tortoise.
> Fly now, you, do fly,
> and bring the clouds together
> for and to the poor farmers.
> Fly, wheel about, . . .
> and come with the clouds at your tails.

Im Hwa, the secretary of KAPF at that time, who was executed by the Communists after the Korean War on the charge of "spying for the United States," had been another important poet of this movement. In an early poem, *Only for You*, he talks about "the sharp wound and angry blood of shame," which the fighters have to face:

> Would there be
> nothing but glory?
> Would there be no shame,
> or wouldn't its name mean it,
> if there were no fight . . . ?
> . . . .
> A fight is the mother
> of both glory and shame,
> it is all of all.
> . . . .
> Because of you, only for you,
> oh battle, I love even humiliation.

A period of furious arguments came to an end as the KAPF members' confidence was gradually shaken. Pak Yŏng-hŭi, a leading critic of the group, who had once argued that "the question is by no means 'how to express,' but it is 'what to express' alone," now made a famous declaration, criticising them in an article published on January 1, 1934: "What we have gained is an ideology, and what we have lost is art itself." This was the year when the Japanese police rounded up KAPF members for the second time, and the organization was practically dissolved.

Apart from the socialistic writers and critics, further development was well under way as the writers set up a system of values, and they had a larger reading public than before. I would say that genuine modern Korean literature was created in the 1930s, during which time aestheticism confronted intellectualism. Of a few new magazines published at the time, the most important one was the *Simunhak* (*Poetic Literature*, 1930–31), which formed what people called the *Simunhak* school of technique or of art for art's sake. The poets of this school paid much attention to the faculties of their language and to poetic craftmanship. The development of aesthetic technique as well as the extended understanding of the notion of "pure poetry" owed a good deal to the introduction of Western literature by Korean students well-informed in English, French, German, and Russian literatures. Imagery became more concrete and fresher, metaphor functioned better, and the music of poetry became more emphatic than ever before. The use of nature images, which has been long traditional, now became rather more personal than nationalistic in its application, and it worked more directly in poetry itself.

Chŏng Chi-yong, one of the outstanding Korean lyricists, must be mentioned here, because he certainly raised the standard of modern Korean poetry in terms of technique, and possibly changed the whole attitude toward the writing of poetry. Having studied English literature in Kyoto, Japan, this Catholic poet, assumed to have been killed during the Korean War, was at his best in commanding intensive diction, with skillfully impacted neologisms at times, fresh images, and solid syntax.

. . . .

and a piebald ox lows vacantly
a golden idle bellow.

. . . .

As ashes in an earthen brazier grow colder
the night wind drives a horse through the field,
                                        Nostalgia
The moment I open the door
the far hills coldly strike my brow.
                                        Spring Snow

The poetic climate of this bright age inspired intellectualism. The theory and criticism along with poetic samples of the intellectualist movement seemed to have encouraged the realm of Korean poetry towards a much more *modern* stage. Credited to this powerful current are the critic Ch'oe Chae-sŏ (1908–64) and the poet-critic Kim Ki-rim. The former, a renowned scholar of English literature, introduced the theories of T. E. Hulme, I. A. Richards, T. S. Eliot, Herbert Read, Aldous Huxley and so forth, and emphasized an objective method in criticism and intellectual approach in writing. Kim Ki-rim, who became the first leader of the modernist movement in Korea, and who also introduced many of the ideas and techniques of twentieth-century Western literature, exercised the theories both in his subtle poetry and in his explicit criticism. His basic principle is that poetry must be intentionally designed, and "poetry is, first of all, a thing to be made." He was not only interested in but often also critical about modern civilization, and what he wanted to build up was the health of Korean poetry.

You the sun,
once will do, I will borrow a crane's throat to call
you. I will level the ruined ground of my mind and
build a small palace for you. Then you, come and
live in it. I will call you my mother . . . .
                                        The Sun's Ways

With emphasis laid on reason, logic and objectivity, the movement brought up such changes as the subject matter of urban life rather than nature, healthy commitment rather than resigned lamentation, conscious and systematic composition rather than spontaneous expression. Intellectualism soon developed into modernism in a broad sense. Some of the participants in the modernist movement, including the surrealistic writer Yi Sang, refreshed the nature of contemporary Korean poetry.

On the other hand, some poets concentrated on seeking for a humanistic approach late in the thirties. The Buddhist-inspired humanist Sŏ Chŏng-ju projected his idea through his poems dealing with lepers, snakes, and cuckoos. *A Leper*, for instance, shows his sympathy for the human being alienated from the world and yet struggling for life: "the leper ate a baby" trying to recover from his disease in accordance with the Korean superstition, "and cried all night." O Chang-hwan, who joined the leftists after 1945 and went to North Korea, used to be this type. "Walking restlessly up and down a ferry all day long, I will feel warm when I hold a passer-by."

At this point, near the end of prewar poetry, yet still far from the end of World War II, I must mention a group of the major poets who first appeared in a monthly called the *Munjang* (*Writings*, 1939–41), in which Chŏng Chi-yong was responsible for bringing new poets. Of a few of "the *Munjang* poets," Pak Tu-jin, Cho Chi-hun, and Pak Mogwŏl shared a common interest in nature, or the Korean tradition, and later came to be known as the "Green Deer" group when the three lyricists' *Green Deer Anthology* was published in 1946. Although they are distinct from each other in many ways, still there is a good reason for putting them together. That is to say, they all attempted to get rid of the chaos and ugliness of the world by seeking the way of corresponding with nature, the flavor and music of their diction being difficult to translate into any other language.

The following observation goes back to their early works. Pak Mogwŏl was absorbed, more than recently, in polishing his language as neatly as "deer" in rhythm somewhat akin to the folk-song.

> A cloud
> circles around
> the clean eyes
> of a green deer.
> *Green Deer*

Most interested in mountains, Pak Tu-jin, a Christian, is often characterized by longing for brightness, as shown in *The Sun*, which is a good example of his favorite repetition of some effective Korean sounds and phrases. "I hate the moon-night . . . over the valleys like tears, . . . over a yard with nobody there. The sun, pretty sun, when you come, . . . I am happy to be with the green hills, their feathers fluttering." Much enriched with the profound background of Buddhism, Cho Chihun manipulated his sensitivity, when he was at his best, in penetrating into and projecting out the stillness of the universe — delicate movement and precise sound, all in quiet — juxtaposed with eternity.

> As I play on the pipe
> in a room under the roof,
> a crane cries on the cloud-way,
> a hundred miles out there.
> *As I Play on the Pipe*

Moving powerfully along with the publication of the many literary magazines in the latter part of the thirties, Korean poetry seemed to have been prepared to work in full flourish. Unfortunately, however, there followed the silent period of Korean literature, as the Japanese invasion of China developed into the Pacific War in 1941, and the use of the Korean language was not allowed in public. Many writers were forced to go underground, while such poets as Yi Yuksa and Yun Tong-ju died in Japanese prisons, the former in Peking and the latter in Hukuoka (Fukuoka), Japan.

The liberation of August 15, 1945, marked a big and surprising change in the history and literature of Korea. All of the poems in Section II of this book were written or published after this date. The Korean language came back, naturally, to full life, but at the same time, unexpectedly, the country was divided by the foreign powers into two parts, alienated from each other. In the South, there immediately emerged literary "fighting" between the adherents of socialist realism and the protectors of pure, national literature, some "neutralistic" people being still sympathetic toward either of the extremes. It was as furious as a political conflict. Most of the younger writers appeared to be concerned with taking a clear standpoint and maintaining their positions through their writings. Within the space of less than five years, the Korean War (1950–53) broke out, and not a few leftist writers went up to the North, whereas others came down to the South around that time.

Here are a couple of examples of war poetry, for which the South Korean poets did not care much, one each from both areas.

A boundary line which cannot be the frontier blocks here,
standing with a knife stabbed in our lungs.

How did the U.S. frontier dare to reach this far?
That's absolutely impossible, inexcusable.

This is an extract from *The Imjin River Blocked* by Cho Pyŏg-am (b. 1908) in North Korea, who used to be in the South, and it is obvious that the poet, appealing to national feelings, condemns the United States for its involvement. On the other hand, a South Korean, Ku Sang, who used to be in the North, forgets about hostility when he stands before the *Enemy's Graves*:

> Being alive, you were related to me
> only with hostility;
> now on the contrary, your resentment
> that you could not vent
> is changed to stay with my hope.
>
> Hearing the gun from somewhere
> I burst into tears before these
> graves of regret and care.

Another poet, Kim Chong-mun, once an officer of the South Korean army, takes a self-analytic attitude toward the war in his *Resistance in June*, and he is not exceptional.

> I have had to live until now
> still as an old soldier
> to resist the countless "I"s,
> someone like myself.

The Korean War, which might have been the start of a bloody battle between the different systems of ideology in the world history, has exercised a tremendous influence on the writing of poetry in the South. Philosophically, it has made some poets come to be attracted by existential and, in part, nihilistic views, and others put more emphasis on humanity; sometimes those viewpoints overlap. Closely related to this, there is one more element to note, which formed another spiritual background: that is, the political ugliness in Korea since 1945. Especially the division of the nation, the leaders' dictatorship and bureaucracy, assassinations and heavy punishments, the ephemeral existence of good leaders, together with social confusions, have led the writers once again back to the sense of transience, detached from reality, although some of them have distinctly committed themselves to the here and now. At the same time, all kinds of disappointment, instability, uneasiness, and anxiety have inspired them to see the world more and more widely.

In technique, these situations helped poets to enrich their poetic devices, subject matter and materials, and to develop indirect expressions. While the arguments between the older and younger generations regarding the Korean tradition and freshness have not always been useless, many of the Korean poets, the younger particularly, have been intentionally and frantically occupied in learning the new trends and techniques of modern Western poetry. As the reader can see in Section II of this collection, a large portion of post-war Korean poetry has many things in common with the West, and the Korean tradition is less parochial than earlier. The only thing we can say, I think, is that some are more conventional and more Korean, and others are more modernistic and universal; this is simply a matter of degree.

There is a little too much complication, and perhaps vagueness too, of stylistic variety and thematic diversity in recent Korean poetry to be described clearly enough in a few lines. Here it seems to me wise to leave it all to the readers, and its evaluation to future consideration.

I want to express my gratitude especially to two poet-professors at The University of Iowa: Paul Engle, who arranged my coming to Iowa on a United States State Department travel grant early in 1964 and my finances thereafter; and Frederic Will, then in charge of the Translation Workshop, who did the enormous amount of work, beyond time and energy, for helping me with his most valuable supervision. Generous, indeed, they have always closely supported this work even after I left Iowa. I am also deeply indebted to the Asia Foundation, both the offices in San Francisco and Seoul, and The JDR 3rd Fund (Porter A. McCray, director), as well as other private funds Paul Engle raised, for their grants which enabled me to carry out the project in Iowa City and Washington, D.C. Without these personal and official aids, I would never have thought of completing this book.

My particular thanks go to The Louis W. and Maud Hill Family Foundation of Saint Paul (A. A. Heckman, executive director), The Iowa Electric Light and Power Company of Des Moines (the late Sutherland Dows, chairman), and to the late Miss Emma Reppert of Santa Barbara (retired school teacher and alumna of The University of Iowa). In a world of many nations, they gave support to writers without regard to nationality.

New York, 1969   Ko Won

Contents

• xxxi •

SECTION II. YOUNGER VOICES: SINCE AUGUST 1945

CONTEMPORARY
KOREAN
POETRY

Section I

Those Windy Nights
1918-1943

CHU YO-HAN (1900–), pseudonym, Songa, studied in both Tokyo and Shanghai, and is a pioneer of modern Korean poetry. Though Ch'oe Nam-sŏn, followed by Yi Kwang-su, made a beginning in writing "new style poetry" before Chu, it was he who first demonstrated "modern" Korean poetry, starting publication in 1919 as a member of the *Ch'angjo* (1919–21), a literary magazine associated with the beginning of romanticism in Korea. His first book of poetry, *Beautiful Dawn*, was published in 1924, and he was a joint author of *Trio Anthology* (1929) in collaboration with Yi Kwang-su and Kim Tong-hwan. In 1960 he was a member of the Korean cabinet.

Chu Yo-han

A SPRING DREAM PASSES

The sun smiles over the new green sprouts,
and the wind rises from the thawing ground,
bringing gently the fragrance of buds
to a melting girl's tender breasts; but,
as bees cast their trembling wings' shadow
and young birds, alighting, shake the branches,
all makes a spring dream only quickly pass.

[1918]   [1924]

HWANG SŎG-U (1895–1959), pen name, Sangat'ap, was involved in the 1920s with such poetry magazines as the *P'yŏhŏ* (1920–21), through which he published symbolistic poems, and *Changmi Ch'on* (1921) and *Chosŏn Sidan* (1928). The last two he founded himself. He published a book of poetry, *Praise for Nature*, in 1929.

Hwang Sŏg-u

HANDING LOVE OVER

The sough of the wind
like the moo of a calf,
like a funeral bell,
comes into the vast moor, covered
under the evening fog like the muddy rain,
incense burning in the graveyard.

Look, my soul is blood-dark like the sky
where flashes the death's lightning.
Lying flat as when Christ prayed at Gethsemane,
listen, it cries, "Free my love back to me."

My soul is the blind, going about an endless
wilderness, much like the thick clouds' inside,
in search of the trace of my only love
who was already with me when I was born.

[1921]

O SANG-SUN (1894–1963), pen name, Kongch'o, a graduate of Dōshisha University, Kyoto, Japan, with a major in religion, first appeared in the poetry magazine *P'yŏhŏ* (1920–21) in 1920. A nihilistic wanderer, never married, he was strongly influenced by Buddhism. A collection of his poetry, *Selected Poems by Kongch'o, O Sang-sun* (1963), came out for the first time only after his death.

O Sang-sun

WANDERING MIND

My soul,
built its nest
on the tide,
oh a nest on the tide . . .

Longing for the sea so eagerly,
sitting on the ground all dried,
I close my eyes, calm down —
then comes the sea to my mind
while time goes unnoticed.

Up in the ruins of a castle,
impatient for the faint, drifting sea
beyond the fields and hills,
and beyond my knowledge of the sunset.

As I call upon the sea in myself
and stare at the waves, again calmly,
the roar from the depth cries
through the tide of my blood.

Now a boundless blue plain of water
spreads out over my inner-eyes,
and the smell of the sea-smoke
condenses at my nose.

[1922]

KIM ŎK (1895– ?), pen name, Ansŏ, is a translator, poet, and journalist, who studied literature at Keiō University, Tokyo, and has translated since 1918 many poetic works from such Western languages as English, French, and Russian, as well as from Chinese. The most important collection of translations is *The Dance of Anguish* (1921). Apart from the first book of his poetry, *The Song of a Jelly-fish* (1923), he wrote almost always in folk-song style. Also he collected in a book the poems of Kim Sowŏl, who was once his student.

Kim Ŏk

FALLING FLOWERS

Why should flowers mind
      what the wind is trying?
They know well they will fall
      when time comes, not forced.

No trees have flowers any more,
      leaves alone are left,
yet the wind still insists —
      unsatisfied with what?

Flowers do not seem, while leaving,
      to blame anybody for a cause,
instead, they are dancing joyfully,
      fluttering in the air.

PYŎN YŎNG-NO (1898–1961), pen name, Suju, a former president of the Korean Center of the International P.E.N. Club, studied at San Jose, California, after he had taught in Seoul. His publications include a book of Korean poetry, *The Mind of Korea* (1924), and a volume of English poems, *Azalea*, besides a *Collection of Essays* and *Korean Odyssey*, both in English.

Pyŏn Yŏng-no

WORRIES

Although you cannot be up there
on a dangerous branch,
still in case, dearest,
I am so worried whenever
a strong wind blows
for I do not know where you are.

[From *The Mind of Korea*, 1924]

HAN YONG-UN (1879–1944), pseudonym, Manhae, a Buddhist monk and one of the thirty-three patriots who had proclaimed Korea's independence in 1919, wrote a number of philosophical and religious poems. Eighty-eight of them were published in a book, *The Silence of My Love* (1926). Besides poetry, he wrote a novel, *The Black Wind*, and was the author of *Restoration of Buddhism* and two other books on Buddhism.

Han Yong-un

OBEYING

Others say, they love freedom, but I choose to obey.

Not that I do not appreciate freedom, but I long only to obey you.

When I do so, obeying is sweeter than beautiful freedom; that is my happiness.

But if you order me to obey someone else, I simply cannot be obedient to you,

for were I to obey him I could be no longer free to obey you.

[From *The Silence of My Love*, 1926]

Han Yong-un

A FERRYBOAT AND A PASSENGER

I am a ferryboat,
you are a passenger.

You tread with muddy feet upon myself.
I go across the water embracing you.
Once I embrace you, I go forward, no matter whether it is deep or
shallow, or swift current.

If you do not come, I wait for you from night to day, remaining
exposed to the wind and snow or rain.
I know you never look back at me when you have ferried over.
Yet I believe you will come soon or later.
Waiting for you, I grow older day by day.

I am a ferryboat,
you are a passenger.

[From *The Silence of My Love*, 1926]

PAK CHONG-HWA (1901–), pen name, Wŏlt'an, one of the major novelists and once president of the Academy of the Arts, published poetry in the *Paekcho* (1922–23), which, with other writers, he established. Besides many novels, his publications include three books of poetry, *Secret Song of the Dark Room* (1924), *Ode on Blue Pottery* (1948), and *Selected Poems* (1961).

Pak Chong-hwa

ODE ON WHITE POTTERY

In the slanting rays of the westerly sun
I stand alone at the window of the museum.

A vase of the Yi Dynasty
of white pottery.
White in color and yet warm,
plain and simple in form.
Truly, truly,
it is a cotton robe
for our fathers and grandfathers
who were mountain hermits.
Good in smell,
broad in mind,
the taste of a simple-minded fool.
How wonderful! Its clouds
of sweet fragrance rise.

In the slanting rays of the westerly sun
I stand alone at the window of the museum.

It has an orchid on it
drawn artlessly with red sand,
and its whiteness is still more delicate;
an old likeness of my mother and grandmother
who were the pride of this locality,
imposing, in sober cotton *chŏgori*
with dangling purple bands.
Its beautiful, fascinating shape and color
should never be allowed to decay.

Oh,
a dignified and generous shape.

chŏgori is a Korean style upper garment.

[1939]

YI SANG-HWA (1900–41) studied French at Tokyo College of Foreign Languages after he had joined the *Paekcho* (1922–23) group. Later he wandered in China. Though he did not write much, his poetry well represents the romanticistic and symbolistic trend of the twenties. A few poems are collected in *Sanghwa and Kowŏl* (1951).

Yi Sang-hwa

TO MY BEDROOM

Madonna, night is returning weary of visits to the worried.
O you, too, run to me before dawn with dew forming on your peach breasts.

Madonna, come to me only in body, leaving all the pearls possessed by the eyes at home.
Let us hurry for we are the two stars that hide themselves when day comes.

Madonna, I am waiting for you trembling with fears in the dark nooks of my mind.
O the first cock crows already, and all dogs are barking. My love, do you hear too?

Madonna, let us go to my bedroom, to the bedroom I made ready all last night.
The old moon is sinking and I hear a footstep — oh, is it yours?

Madonna, look at the short-wicked candle of my beseeching mind fighting back the tear.
It is so feeble, it will be choked to faint smoky death even in the woolly wind.

Madonna, let us go now; a shadow without feet is coming near like a ghost from the hill out front.
O someone may see . . . my heart throbs, my love, I call you.

Madonna, it will soon dawn. Come here right away before a temple
   bell laughs at us.
Cling to my neck, let us go, we too, to the long-affecting land with
   this night.

Madonna, no one may enter my bedroom across the log bridge of
   regret and fear.
O the breeze comes. Come as lightly as that. My love, are you
   coming now?

Madonna, what a pity. Am I mad to hear a sound which cannot
   be true?
I am burning as if all the blood of my body and the spring of my
   heart have dried up.

Madonna, sooner or later we must go. Why don't we go, then, of
   our free will, not dragged?
You are my *Maria* who believes in my word, who knows
   my bedroom as a cave of resurrection.

Madonna, there is no difference among night dreams, those we
   construct, and the dreams of life with which man struggles.
O let us go to my bedroom, which doesn't care for time like a
   child's heart, to the beautiful and long-affecting land.

Madonna, the laughter of the stars is going to fade away, and the
   waves of night are also becoming dry.
O you must come to me before the fog clears. My love, I call you.

[1918]   [1919]

Yi Sang-hwa

THE LAMENTATION OF A CORRUPT AGE

Down to a bloody evening cave,
oh to that bottomless cave,
not knowing an end,
no end,
I will fall prone
and will be buried there.

In the sick heart of autumn,
right in the dreaming heart,
not caring about
day or night,
I will push my drunken body up
and will brew a bitter laugh.

[1922]

HONG SA-YONG (1900–47), pen name, Nojak, an active participant in the *Paekcho* (1922–23), a magazine edited by him for the romanticist group in the twenties, was a most sentimental "king of tears" as he claimed in a poem, *I Am a King* (1922). He was also a leading member of the drama society, T'owŏl-hoe.

Hong Sa-yong

MOOD OF A LASS

A shaggy dog dozes
    on a slope in the field,
the queer wind affects
    the mood of a lass.

Rend down a branch
of a willow for me.
O, don't break it off
but wrench away.

No use in plucking
the withering herbs.
    Ninana na . . .
    Nanana ni . . .

[1922]

KIM TONG-HWAN (1901– ?), pen name, P'ain, a journalist and publisher of the *Samch'ŏlli* magazine, studied literature at Tōyō University, Tokyo. He wrote the first Korean epic, *The Night on the Border* (1925); also published are *Youth Ascending to Heaven* (1925), and other books of poetry which mostly come from folk sources. He was taken to the North during the Korean War and his present-day life is not known. His wife Ch'oe Chŏng-hŭi, a writer, lives in Seoul.

Kim Tong-hwan

BLAME FOR A SMILE

Asked a short cut
    I answered him.
Asked for some water,
    drew it from the well.
And then with a smile
    accepted his thanks.

May the sun never rise —
    goodness knows.
I did nothing to blame,
    but just smiled.

[From *Trio Anthology*, 1929]

KIM P'ALBONG (1903–), given name, Ki-jin, a novelist, critic, and poet, and a former member of the *Paekcho*, studied English literature at Rikkyō University in Tokyo, and became the leader of PASCULA and KAPF, organizations of the proletarian arts in the twenties. His novels include *The Sound of the Tide*, *Re-start*, *The Young Man Kim Ok-kyun*, and *The United World*.

Kim P'albong

LAMENTATION OF THE WHITE HANDS

Easy at chairs in a café, boasting
of the white arms, here are the young
Russians of sixty years past,
shouting "V NAROD."

Café-chair revolutionists,
your hands are too white.

Only in a saying, "V NAROD!" . . .
proud of the white arms, the useless
lamentation of the young Russians
of sixty years past is still with us.
Café-chair revolutionists,
your hands are too white.

You are the "white hands" —
meaningless to those farmers
who want to advance
and who have little "gustration."
You are the café-chair revolutionists.

"The lamentation of the white hands"
of the young Russians, sixty years ago,

must have been a hard sign of wishing
to go out for their commitment,
forgetting about the taste of good food.

Café-chair revolutionists,
your hands are too white.

[1924]

YANG CHU-DONG (1903–), pen name, Muae, a graduate of Waseda, Tokyo, with a major in English, is a renowned professor of Korean classics at Tongguk. He founded two literary magazines in the twenties: the *Kŭmsŏng* (1923), and the *Munye Kongnon* (1929), and wrote both poetry and criticism. Besides important studies in old Korean poetry, he published a book of verse, *The Pulse of Korea* (1932), a book of translations from modern British and American poetry, and another from the poetry of T. S. Eliot.

Yang Chu-dong

A SHORT PIECE

Look at those two white birds
flying in the blue sky. You see,
life is light and movement, and
the harmony of the two.

Where are the birds gone? —
there into the clouds.
Now a flower is falling,
of itself, in the front yard.

Listen to the blossoms all crying
as they roll down over the ground.
Death is sound and standstill, and
the shudder of the two, you see.

[1922]

YI CHANG-HŬI (1902–28), pen name, Kowŏl, was educated in Kyoto, Japan, and became a leading symbolist in Korea during the 1920s. His pessimism led him to commit suicide by taking poison at the age of twenty-six. His posthumous works were published in a book compiled by Paek Ki-man, *Sanghwa and Kowŏl* (1951).

Yi Chang-hŭi

THE BREASTS OF THE BLUE SKY

The warm spring flows on
in the blue sky which I
choose to call innocently
mother, mother.
She shows her big breasts
shining in white, more beautiful
than a bunch of dewy grapes.

Look at the charming breasts.
O sweet milk seems to fall in drops.
One cannot help but cry for it,
thirst for it, right this moment.
A thoughtless appetite,
the fat and good-looking breasts . . .
Lonely soul, fly up like an arrow,
rise high to the clear sky.

[1922]

Yi Chang-hŭi

SPRING IS A CAT

A fragrance of spring loiters
in the cat's fur as tender as pollen.

The flame of mad spring blazes
in the cat's eyes like golden bells.

A gentle drowsiness of spring floats
on the cat's lips closed calm.

The sap of green spring leaps
in the cat's whiskers stretched sharp.

[1923]

KIM SOWŎL (1903–34), given name, Chŏng-sik, once a student at Tokyo Commercial College, first appeared in the *Kaebyŏk* in 1922, and has since published a large number of folk-song-type lyrics in the *Yŏngdae* (1924) and other magazines. His first book, *Azaleas*, was published in 1925. More than ten different editions of his poetry, under such titles as *Invocation*, *Sanyuhwa* and *Azaleas*, have been widely read by the present-day public.

Kim Sowŏl

AZALEAS

When you leave, tired of me,
I will be ready to let you go,
no complaints, whatsoever.

And I will carpet your way
with azaleas, armfuls,
from the familiar Yaksan hill.

May you enjoy light steps
on the flowers for your path
as you go ahead, if you like.

When you leave, tired of me,
I surely won't cry,
no tears, never.

[1922]

Kim Sowŏl

YEARNING

The road is dusky under the sunset.
Over the dark mountains the clouds are lost.
My love will not come even late,
yet, even so, my yearning is greater.
Whom should I go to meet and where?
The moon is rising, wild geese cry in the air.

[1925]

CHŎNG CHI-YONG (1903– ?), one of the most aesthetic and influential poets of modern Korea, studied English literature at Dōshisha University in Kyoto, Japan, and has published poetry since 1927. He deserves much credit for developing "pure poetry" in the 1930s, mainly through the *Simunhak* (1930–31), a powerful poetry magazine, with his highly polished poetic diction and fresh imagery, for which some people of the time attacked him as a mere "technician." He was also responsible for finding and bringing out a few talented younger poets in the *Munjang*. He published *Collected Poems* (1935), *The White Deer Cascade* (1941), *Selected Poems*, and *Proses*. He was assumedly killed during the Korean War.

Chŏng Chi-yong

NOSTALGIA

To the east end of large fields
an old-tale-chattering brook meanders out,
and a piebald ox lows vacantly
a golden idle bellow.
— Even in a dream it remains in me.

As ashes in an earthen brazier grow colder
the night wind drives a horse through the field,
and my old father tired by a dusky drowsiness
raises his straw pillow.
— Even in a dream it remains in me.

I, with a soil-grown mind,
was getting wet to the skin with the grass-dew
looking for an arrow which I shot carelessly
aiming at the long sky's blue.
— Even in a dream it remains in me.

Young sister, flying hair down the lobes
like the waves that dance on the fabled sea,
and my barefoot wife, the ordinary,
gathered ears of corn against the blazing sun.
— Even in a dream it remains in me.

In the sky the dense stars
step towards a mysterious sand castle,
over a poor roof the frosty crows pass cawing,
by the lamplight people chat in a circle.
— Even in a dream it remains in me.

[1925]   [1927]

Chŏng Chi-yong

LAKE

A face simply
can be hidden
with two palms . . .

But the desire to see
so large as the lake,
there is nothing for it
but to close my eyes.

[From *Poems by Chŏng Chi-yong*, 1934]

Chŏng Chi-yong

SPRING SNOW

The moment I open the door
the far hills coldly strike my brow.

Right on the first day
of the early spring month.

My forehead confronts, cool and bright,
the still snow-covered peak.

The cracked ice and new wind following
make my white coat-tie smell good.

It is now like a dream, rather sad,
to have had such a shrinking time.

Parsley sprouts green,
the once motionless fishes mumble.

For the unseasonable snow before flowering
I long to be cold again without warm clothes.

IM HWA (1908–53), a former secretary and leading poet-critic of KAPF, had been active in the leftist movement in the South until he joined the North Korean Communists. He was killed by them on the charge of being an "American spy." He published three books of poetry in Seoul, including *Hyŏnhaet'an* (1938) and *Praises* (1947), in addition to a collection of his essays, *The Logic of Literature* (1940), and edited anthologies of *Modern Korean Poetry* and *Korean Folksongs.*

Im Hwa

BECAUSE OF YOU, ONLY FOR YOU

Would there be
nothing but glory?
Would there be no shame,
or wouldn't its name mean it,
if there were no fight . . . ?

If there were no fight, in fact,
there would be neither of them.
A fight is the mother
of both glory and shame,
it is all of all.

What makes the blood of defeat
brew the wine of victory,
and what makes humiliation
draw out perfumes of glory,
is the vast sea of a fight.

Without limit,
that sea is where
victory enjoys most
fishing the pearls of its pleasure,
and defeat realizes most bitterly
the high value of its sufferings.

It is the very sea where
the sharp wound and angry blood
of shame, which is not easily cleared,
all bloom like the red roses.
(You, friends, must know
what the word shame means.)

Because of you, only for you,
oh battle, I love even humiliation.

[1938]

PAEK KI-MAN (1901–69) studied at Waseda, Tokyo, and published poetry in the twenties, which he later included in *Sanghwa and Kowŏl* (1951), primarily a collection of his two friends' poems. He was once put in prison by the Japanese after the Independence Movement of 1919, and later wandered many places until 1945.

Paek Ki-man

GREEN FROG

The green frog croaks in a long rainy weather. By the coldly wet trees, looking up grievously at the sky, he cries and cries only until he cannot.

The green frog was a bad son. He never listened to his mother. When she told him to go to the hill and play, he went instead to the river. He did things the other way round.

When the much troubled mother-frog was facing death, she wanted to be buried up in the hill. So she thought out quite the opposite, and asked the poor child, patting him on the head, to bury her body by the river when she died.

The death of his mother shocked him like a thunderclap. He suffered for the first time from a painful penitence for his disobedient past.

With his little heart full of sorrow, now he was ready to follow his mother's last words. He buried her dead body by the clean stream. Falling down on the tomb, stamping his feet, he wailed.

Ever since, everytime when it keeps raining, he has been worried about her grave, much worried about the evil muddy water, the damned flood.

That is why the green frog croaks in the long rainy weather. Thinking of his mother's grave in grief, he can do nothing but cry at the top of his voice, sadly, sadly — without eating and sleeping.

[1921]

KIM HYŎNG-WŎN (1901–), pen name, Sŏksong, a renowned journalist, was particularly interested in Walt Whitman's poetry, and published his poems most in the *Kaebyŏk* (1920–26). He was taken to the North during the Korean War.

Kim Hyŏng-wŏn

BREATHING MUMMY

Here I see
a breathing mummy.

A mummy that is
dressed in *modern times,*
embalmed with *system,*
and laid in the coffin of *life.*

And I lament, alas,
over myself who is already
nothing but
a breathing mummy.

[1922]

YI ŬN-SANG (1903–), pen name, Nosan, one of the most impor-
tant *sijo* writers, studied at Yŏnhŭi College (Yŏnse University) and
Waseda, Tokyo. He first published poetry in the modern style, later
concentrating on the *sijo* tradition. His numerous publications in-
clude *Collected Sijos by Nosan* (1934, 1939), *Selected Sijos by
Nosan* (1958), *Selected Writings of Nosan* (1964), and studies in
history.

Yi Ŭn-sang

SŎNGBUL TEMPLE
(*sijo*)

Deep night at the Sŏngbul-sa,
        the wind-bell muffles its chiming.
A visitor listens by himself
        while the monk is sleeping.
Let the guest sleep too
        so the bell cries alone.

With each sound, he fears,
        it may jingle again;
when it stops, he grows nervous
        waiting for another.
With the wind-bell ringing,
        he cannot sleep all night.

[1931]

YI PYŎNG-GI (1891–1967), pen name, Karam, a prominent *sijo* writer, was a professor of Korean classic literature, and a member of the Academy of the Arts. He published *Collected Sijos by Karam* (1939, 1947), and *The History of Korean Literature* in collaboration with Paek Ch'ŏl.

Yi Pyŏng-gi

DEAD LOVE
(*sijo*)

The night my love left
    comes back every year.
Cocks crow as sadly
    as this particular time.
The setting moon is red
    like eyes after weeping.

KIM YŎNG-JIN (1899–), pen name, Nasan or Chŏknasanin, studied at Tōyō University, Tokyo, and has published both *sijo* poetry and literary criticism.

Kim Yŏng-jin

AN OLD MIRROR
(*sijo*)

Bright as the moon, I understand,
this one used to mirror a beauty.
In those days when she was there,
how could it ever have a mote?
Though it is cracked and rusty,
still I feel like seeing my love.

[1939]

KIM HAEGANG (1903–), given name, Tae-jun, published poems mostly in the late twenties and thirties, and they were collected in *Blue Horse* (1940) in collaboration with Kim Namin. He also wrote some serialized fiction for newspapers.

Kim Haegang

THE MOON AT THE DIAMOND MOUNTAIN

The beautiful mountains and the moon
project the night so serene,
a lazy mountain-visitor feels fresh.

The water by the window
under the Milky Way sounds clean
as I make the image of the moon my pillow.

Eyes opened, I see over there
the vivid face at the mountain brow.
When I close eyes, then I hear
the moon breaking, knocked by the water.

I simply cannot sleep,
no need for talk,
facing the moon by myself.

Through that mirror, mind is illuminated.
I wish to worship it, deep at night,
somewhat like Buddha.

[1940]

KIM TONG-MYŎNG (1901–68) majored in theology at Aoyama Gakuin, Tokyo, and came from North Korea after 1945. He published five books of verse, including *My Harp* (1930), *Plantian* (1938), and *The Pearl Harbor* (1954). For the latter he was awarded the Asia Foundation's Free Literature Prize in 1954. He also wrote many articles of political criticism.

Kim Tong-myŏng

MY MIND IS

My mind is a lake:
come and row, I pray you.
On the sides of your boat I'll break,
embracing your white image, bijou.

My mind is a candlelight:
will you please shut the door?
Trembling quiet at your silken skirt
I'll burn to the last, till no more.

My mind is a traveller:
please play on a flute.
I'll keep going all the lonely night,
lend you my ear in the moonlight.

My mind is a falling leaf:
let me stay for a while in your garden.
When the wind rises, I'll travel again,
in solitude I'll leave you.

Kim Tong-myŏng

THE RIVER FLOWS

The river flows,
and I stand by the riverside whistling.

The season flies in lightly like a kingfisher,
and unnamed plants flower by the riverside.

The season flies off lightly like a kingfisher,
and the unnamed plants fall by the riverside.

White clouds come across the river like sheep,
and the man who stands on the bank is no longer me.

White clouds go across the river like sheep,
and the man who stands on the bank is another me.

The river flows,
and I disappear from the riverside whistling.

[From *The Sky*, 1948]

PAK YONG-CH'ŎL (1904–38), pen name, Yonga, studied at Yŏnhŭi College (now Yŏnse University) in Seoul and Aoyama Gakuin in Tokyo. He made a great contribution to the development of modern poetry through the establishment and editing of such magazines as the *Simunhak* (1930–31), *Munye Wŏlgan* (1931–32), and *Munhak* (1933). Besides *Collected Poems* (1939), many of his poems, translations, and criticisms are included in the *Complete Works of Pak Yong-ch'ŏl* in two volumes.

Pak Yong-ch'ŏl

DEPARTING BOAT

I am sailing too.
Why should I waste
my youth crying here?
I am leaving too.

Hard to get away from the cosy port,
the wet and foggy eyes stick on it.
So with those I love, even their wrinkles
I am familiar with as with every line of the hills.

One who has to leave, being driven, and people
he leaves behind, all will be long remembered.
The wind plays with the clouds as I look back.
No place prepared ahead for my entrance.

Yet I am sailing.
Why should I waste
my youth crying here?
I am leaving too.

[1939]

KIM YŎNGNANG (1903–50), given name, Yun-sik, attended Aoyama Gakuin, Tokyo, and became a contributor for the *Simunhak* in 1930, demonstrating his aestheticism. His quotation from Keats, "A thing of beauty is a joy forever" in his first book of *Poems by Yŏngnang* (1935) may suggest his interest. *Selected Poems* was published in 1949.

Kim Yŏngnang

TILL THE PEONY BLOOMS

Till the peony blooms
I will still be waiting for my spring.
On the day when the peony petals drop
I will drown in the sorrow of losing spring.
Once in May, sultry hours,
when even the fallen petals had died
and every trace of peony had vanished,
my fruitful outflow was blighted.
As a peony falls, a year of mine goes, all go.
I cry through all its day with sorrow.
Till the peony blooms I will be still
waiting for the brilliant sadness of spring.

[From *Poems by Yŏngnang*, 1935]

Kim Yŏngnang

DRUM

You sing the song, I will take the drum.

Chinyangjo, Chungmŏri, Chungjungmŏri, Utmŏri,
any song in fine melody, in one phrase,
a perfect harmony of breathing.
It is rare, in pain or delight.

Once separate from its sound,
a drum is merely a skin. If I miss my beat
you must change your breathing.

Not enough to say that the drum beats time,
more than the accompaniment sustaining the song,
it is rather the conductor.

I am the great drummer, forget the little tune.
Boom-boom. Still in motion, silent in sound.
Life ripens in its autumn.

You sing the song, I will beat the drum.

[From *Selected Poems*, 1949]

YI HA-YUN (1906–), pen name, Yŏnp'o, a professor, translator, anthologist, and poet, majored in English at Hōsei University, Tokyo, and participated in the Foreign Literature Research Society, which published the journal *Haeoe Munhak* in 1927. Formerly the vice-president of the Korean National Commission for UNESCO, he teaches at Seoul University. His publications include a book of poetry, *Water Mill* (1939), and translations of British, Irish, and French poetry, besides a few anthologies of contemporary Korean poetry, including *Modern Lyrics* (1939).

Yi Ha-yun

A WATER MILL

A water mill is rolling on and on
with the leaves of recollection I gather.
Each leaf of memory clings to the wheel
as water pushes it in and out.

The wheel turning and shouting
draws my mind back to the past,
which only wets and pounds my thoughts.

. . . .

And look, the grey-haired miller,
what do his tired eyes seek for?
Water flows down with no pause,
while the pestle is pounding hard, noisily.

[1930]

KIM KWANG-SŎP (1906–), pen name, Isan, a graduate of Waseda, Tokyo, with a major in English, participated in the Foreign Literature Research Society (established in 1926), the Dramatic Arts Society, and the poetry magazine, *Siwŏn* (1935). His poetry shows calmness all through his four books, *Aspiration* (1938), *Mind* (1949), *Sunflower* (1957), and *Dove in Sŏngbuk-tong* (1969).

Kim Kwang-sŏp

UNSEEN STAR

For whom do I wait
here by the candlelight?
After Time was forgotten
stars appear to the sight.

Look, strangers pass through,
walking a narrow path by me.
Do you stars remember everybody
who goes by looking at you?

Morning reminds me of the thick spring
like the leaves when they are growing;
but when the evening light goes away
nostalgia holds sway, near me.

Is there any other star
beyond them, unseen to all?
It may be there that I shall fall
where the light cannot reach.

Kim Kwang-sŏp

TAKE YOURSELF AWAY

Take yourself away from me.
Even if the mark you leave may smart
take yourself away from my heart.

For my mind goes where you have gone
and love makes a deep sigh,
and still I pass you by.

Believing one day we will be together
I recall the day I dismissed you, in vain.
In my tears you pass, go again.

SIN SŎK-CHŎNG (1907–) studied Buddhism, which influenced his poetry. In the early 1930s, he contributed to the *Simunhak* magazine with highly lyrical poems, and later published three volumes of poetry, *Candlelight* (1939), *The Sad Idyl* (1947), and *Glacier* (1956).

Sin Sŏk-chŏng

LITTLE ANIMALS

Nan and I together
liked to watch the sea from the hill.
Through the space of the sparse trees,
— chestnuts, pines,
oaks and elms,
the sea looked bluer than the sky.

She and I,
sitting like little animals,
took pleasure in watching the sea
quietly like animals, like the water.

When she and I, facing the sea,
up and down the stairs of red coral
and white marble, set by the clouds over again,
felt the celadon islands floating like ducks,
I saw the elm leaves cling to her hair
scattering as a heart shakes.

Nan and I,
still sitting quietly under the elms,
were gentle little animals looking at the sea.

[1939]

Sin Sŏk-chŏng

IF YOU CALL ME

As gingko leaves, yellowed in autumn,
dance and toss in the wind,
    so I will come to you
    if you call me, my love.

As the new moon moves over the hills silently
at night when a lake is veiled in mist,
    so I will come to you
    if you call me, my love.

As the water meanders at the edge of heaven
under the soft-melted spring sky,
    so I will come to you
    if you call me, my love.

As the sun soaks into the lawn in early season
when egrets sing out through the bright air,
    so I will come to you
    if you call me, my love.

[From *Candlelight*, 1939]

Sin Sŏk-chŏng

THE DAFFODILS

The daffodils
in a white bowl are closed like young lotus.

The daffodils
are embraced by a white bowl shaped like a hen.

The daffodils
have growing buds as frail as the chick's beak.

The daffodils may grow in stone and water,
but are not such cold-blooded plants.

They strive to lick the spring time
with the green tips of their tongues.

[From *The Sad Idyl*, 1947]

KIM KI-RIM (1909–), pen name, P'yŏnsŏkch'on, a graduate of Tōhoku University, Japan, was the first leader of intellectualism and the early modernist movement in the thirties, during which he introduced many theories and techniques of modern Western literature, and criticized all the romantistic sentimentalists of the time. He wrote his poetry under some influence of the early works of Pound and Eliot. He came to the South after the liberation, and was taken captive by the North Korean Army during the Korean War. His publications include *Weather-map* (1936), *The Sun's Way* (1939), *The Sea and Butterfly, New Song,* and criticism *On Poetry,* and *Introduction to Literature.*

Kim Ki-rim

WINDOW-GLASS AND MIND

Look,
my mind seems glass — it clouds easily,
like the winter air, at the slightest sigh.

Reaction to my touch looked hard as iron,
but it is cracked only in the frost of a night.

When snow storms, it shouts and cries.
On the night's retreat, tears wet the cheeks.

Passion that cannot catch fire; a lighthouse for the bats.
It passes all night, looking up enviously at a flying star.

Look,
my mind seems glass —
it breaks this easily even in the moonlight.

[1935]

Kim Ki-rim

THE SUN'S WAYS

You the sun,
once will do, I will borrow a crane's throat to call you. I will
    level the ruined ground of my mind and build a small palace
    for you. Then you, come and live in it. I will call you my
    mother, my home, my love, my hope. And will bite this
    darkness to death, with your strength.

You the sun,
lick clean last night's frost from the lake, hills, green lawn and
    white bank in the tiny world of my heart. Pass your hands
    over my brook, swing my cradle of the sea. Visit my sick-
    room like a cheerful guest bringing the fish-like morning.

For the light in my dark sick-room, I have poetry which is less
    lovely than the sun, sad poetry which cannot be the sun, and
    am waiting for your coming without sleep all this night, you
    the sun.

[1939]

Kim Ki-rim

THE SEA AND BUTTERFLY

No one has ever told her about the depth,
a white butterfly is never afraid of the sea.

Down to the blue, taking it for a garden,
she brines her faint wings in the waves
and comes back like an exhausted princess.

Sadder, no ocean flowers in early spring.
The young moon is cold at her waist.

KIM SANG-YONG (1902–51), pseudonym, Wŏlp'a, a graduate of Rikkyō University, Tokyo, with a major in English, also studied at Boston University and taught college in Seoul. He published a book of poetry, *Viewing Home* (1939).

Kim Sang-yong

I WILL MAKE A WINDOW

I will make a window
to the sunny south.
It's the time to plough.
I'm going to hoe up and weed.

The cloud cannot lure me to leave here.
I would prefer the birds' song free.
When the corn is ripe, why don't you
come and eat it with me?

Should you ask why I live,
I would smile.

[From *Viewing Home*, 1939]

MO YUN-SUK (1910–), pen name, Yŏngun, a graduate of Ewha Women's College (Now Ewha University), first appeared in the *Siwŏn*, a poetry magazine published in 1935. She published five volumes of lyrical poetry: the first, *Bright Area* (1933), and the latest, *Waves* (1951). She has been actively engaged in cultural and women's organizations.

Mo Yun-suk

AUTUMN MAPLES

The dream is still green,
alive in the lively land,
raising up the fallen heart, and
glancing loneliness is beautiful again.
The fog-dimmed breast
waits for the night
as gently as the evening sky.
Stars, stars.
You come to me silently.

But hope fails in isolation
on a slope of fading maples,
while the wind blows uselessly, and blows:
a day of branches too lonely to sing,
and the cry of autumn birds rings
on the dark leaves by the deserted path.

[From *Bijou Pinyŏ*, 1947]

YU CH'I-HWAN (1908–67), pen name, Ch'ŏngma, attended Yŏnhŭi College and started publishing poetry in the *Munye Wŏlgan* (1931–32) in 1931. Eleven volumes of his verse include *Poems by Ch'ŏngma* (1939), *Book of Life* (1947), *Diary of a Dragon-Fly* (1949), and *Eastern Zelkova* (1959). He was awarded both The City of Seoul Cultural Prize (1950) and The Asia Foundation's Free Literature Prize (1958).

Yu Ch'i-hwan

FLAG

This is a voiceless shouting;
a handkerchief of everlasting nostalgia
waving for that expansion of the blue sea.
Its innocence flaps in the wind like waves,
and sorrow outstretches its wings like an egret
at the stafftop of the pure and upright thought.
O who was it,
who was so clever as to hang first
this sad and touching mind in the air?

[1936]

Yu Ch'i-hwan

ROCK

When I die, I long to become a rock:
which is never infected with love or pity,
remains unmoved by joy and anger;
is beaten by the rain and the wind,
keeping the insentient silence forever,
whipping its own inside
until it even forgets about life;
a rock which does not sing, if it dreams,
under the flowing clouds
and the far-off thunders,
nor cries out even if broken to pieces.
I long to become such a rock.

NO CH'ŎN-MYŎNG (1913–57) started publishing her poetry while she was attending Ewha Women's College, and was a member-contributor for the *Siwŏn* magazine. She published five volumes of verse, including *Coral Forest* (1938), *Around the Window* (1945), *The Song of Deer* (1958), and two collections of miscellaneous writings.

No Ch'ŏn-myŏng

DEER

Because of your long neck
you are a sad animal;
always quiet and gentle.
Your line must have been of high birth,
you have their noble crown.
Looking at your image in the water
brings back long lost tales
with a nostalgia too sharp to bear.
You look over, stretching your sad neck
toward the far hill.

[From *Coral Forest*, 1938]

No Ch'ŏn-myŏng

CRICKET

Because my shelter must not be known,
because my poorness must not show,
in hiding through the night I cry.
For somewhere someone weeps like me
I must soak more in the moonlight,
retain the sorrow of my night again
there behind the stone steps.

[From *Coral Forest*, 1938]

IM HAK-SU (1911–) graduated from Seoul University with an English major and has taught college. He published five volumes of poetry, including *Pomegranate* (1937) and *Migratory Birds* (1939), in addition to a book of translations, *Modern English Poetry* (1939).

Im Hak-su

TWILIGHT

A faint mural painting has begun to move
telling us the long story of mankind.

It steps like the shadow of the moon
that swims in a lake. On the cheeks,
pale and strained, flow down
tossing life and eternal rhythm.
The closed lips wish to pass another day
dreaming from one flower to another.

Hair is like the evening sea with no wind
under the horizon of broken memories.
In the slight fear of a universe that is
beyond solution, the brow is lost in worries.
And yet, the eyes droop shyly
in the joy of love, coming late finally.

While the westerly sun colors
the sky and earth in rose-red finely,
here Venus of a thousand years past,
unchanged, has toddled out to marble.

KIM KWANG-GYUN (1914–), one of the major "modernists" of the thirties' "new generation," is characterized by visualization of anxieties of the modern world. He published three volumes of poetry, including *Gaslight* (1939) and *Twilight Song* (1957).

Kim Kwang-gyun

A SNOWY NIGHT

Scattering silently in the dead of night,
is it a sweet word from somewhere distant?
Snow falls like a plaintive old trace
when an oil lamp grows thin at the eaves.

The white breaths make me feel heavy,
and I alone go out to the dark garden
with a lamp in my airy mind.

Rustle of a woman undressing far away.

The dim snowflakes:
are they the pieces of a certain lost memory?
Cold regret makes me annoyingly uneasy.

Dressed icily, again alone,
with no light nor fragrance at all,
snow falls and lies on.
And my sadness condenses on it.

[From *Gaslight*, 1939]

Kim Kwang-gyun

GASLIGHT

A gloomy lamp hangs on the empty air.
Quiet signal for me to go — where alone?

A long summer day folded its wings in haste,
twilight humidifies buildings like tombstones,
glittering night is tangled like thick weeds,
and my thoughts are all numbed.

Darkness soaks in through my skin.
Shouting of the strange streets.
I am moved to tears, I don't know why.

From where did I carry such a burden of sorrow,
getting between the rows of blank crowds?
How dark this long laid shadow!

What quiet signal for me, how and where to?
A gloomy lamp hangs on the empty air.

[From *Gaslight*, 1939]

O ILTO (1902–46), given name, Hŭi-byŏng, majored in philosophy at Rikkyō University, Tokyo. He published poems in the thirties, during which he founded and edited a poetry magazine, the *Siwŏn* (1935).

O Ilto

MY GIRL

Where has my girl gone?
On an empty branch
is hung a basket alone.

. . . .

The light silken haze
flickers before the tree
today again after days.

KIM O-NAM (1906–), a graduate of Japan Women's University with a major in English, is one of a very few women writers of the *sijo*, and has been concentrating on the tradition since the early 1930s. She published two books of poetry in this form, *Sijos* (1952), and *Image of Mind* (1956).

Kim O-nam

WHO SAID
(*sijo*)

Who said living in solitude
was far too lonely?
The silhouette of an oil lamp
fondly keeps company.
When I wipe my tears,
it does so with me.

[1934]

YI YUKSA (1905–44), given name, Hwal, a graduate of Peking University, died in Peking prison where he was confined by the Japanese while he was revisiting China shortly before Korea's liberation. His first book of poetry, *Green Grapes* (1940), was followed by the posthumous publication, *Poems by Yuksa* (1956).

Yi Yuksa

THE WIDE PLAIN

In the ancient times
when the heaven was first open,
no cock might have been heard to crow.

None of the high mountains,
all rushing out to the longed sea,
could have dared invade this land.

While busy seasons were blowing and
fading with endless time,
a great river first made the way.

Now the snow falls,
and plum blossoms alone smell far away.
Let me sow the seeds of my poor song here.

And, let a superman who may come
on a white horse, a million years later again,
sing out the songs aloud in this wide plain.

[1940]

YI SANG (1910–37), real name, Kim Hae-gyŏng, majored in architecture at Seoul College of Engineering. He wrote both poetry and fiction in the 1930s, most of which was surrealistic and difficult to understand. He was arrested by the Japanese police, and died in Japan. His posthumous writings are published in the *Collected Works of Yi Sang* (1956) in three volumes.

Yi Sang

A MIRROR

No sound in the mirror.
Any other world may not be that quiet.

I have my ears in the mirror too,
poor ears that do not understand my word.

The I in the mirror is a left-hander,
who neither accepts nor knows a hand-shake.

But for the mirror how could I even see him
although I do not feel him because of it?

No mirror with me at the moment, but he is
always there. He may now be working hard alone.

He is exactly opposite, yet so similar to me.
Only sorry, I cannot examine or help him.

[1933]

KIM TAL-CHIN (1907–), a graduate of Hehwa College, is one of the most Buddhistic poets of this century. He first appeared in the *Siwŏn* in 1934; a book of poetry, *Green Persimmon*, was published in 1940. Besides teaching, he is enaged in translating the Buddhist texts into modern Korean.

Kim Tal-chin

A PRISONER

I've been waiting for something, somewhere,
things like a red rose, a white dove,
a dewy field in the fresh May morning,
or the bright sunshine; — for something
with which my life can be crystallined.

Sitting by a large building's window
where the shadow flickers after the snow,
I look out at the streets of Seoul
depressed under the moody sky.

And I alone think of a prisoner:
someone locked up somewhere in my mind's corner
falling down exhausted, like the Seven Sleepers,
having no day or night from time immemorial.

SŎ CHŎNG-JU (1915–), a member of the Academy of the Arts, studied at Hehwa College, and founded in 1936 a poetry magazine, the *Siin Purak*, to which O Chang-hwan, Ham Hyŏng-su, and Kim Tong-ni contributed. He is now teaching at Tongguk University, and has published four volumes of poetry, including *Flowery Snakes* (1941) and *The Silla Poems* (1959), in addition to anthologies and translations.

Sŏ Chŏng-ju

LEPER

Sad about the sun and the sky-blue.
So much it had been with the leper,

when the moon rose at the barley field,
there he ate a baby, and cried all night —

that was a cry as red as a flower.

[From *Flowery Snakes*, 1941]

Sŏ Chŏng-ju

BESIDE A CHRYSANTHEMUM

To bring a chrysanthemum to flower
the cuckoo may have cried
since spring.

Again, to bring a chrysanthemum to flower
the thunder must have rolled
behind black clouds.

Long ago in the backways of youth
your heart languished in love and longing;
now you are in bloom, much like my sister,
standing before the mirror.

To force your yellow flowers
it may have had to frost last night;
I could not sleep at all.

Sŏ Chŏng-ju

SWING SONG
(Ch'unhyang's words)

Hyangdan, push the swing.
As if to push off a boat
for the distant sea.
Hyangdan, my maid.

From this swaying weeping willow,
from the embroidery of flowers as on a pillow,
and from the nightingales and butterflies,
Hyangdan, push me away.

To that sky without coral or islands,
push me up,
up like the colored clouds.
Push my leaping heart up.

Try as I may I cannot go
as the moon goes to the West.

Push me up
as the wind pushes up the waves,
Hyangdan, my maid.

Ch'unhyang: the heroine of the anonymous novel, the *Ch'unhyang Chŏn*,
written sometime in the late eighteenth century. The daughter of a socially
degraded *kisaeng*, or professional woman entertainer, she is a popular ex-
ample of a pretty, virtuous, and faithful young lady.

CHANG MAN-YŎNG (1914–), pen name, Ch'oae, is one of those who were under the influence of the modernist movement in the thirties. His publications include the *Sheep* (1937), *Festival* (1939), *Selected Poems* (1964), and two other books of poetry.

Chang Man-yŏng

THE MOON, GRAPES, LEAVES

Look, Suni, the tide of moon surged in
to an archaic garden, insects singing.

The moon quietly sat in my yard.
She is more fragrant than a fruit.

Autumn night,
blue like the East Sea.

The pretty grapes soak up the moonlight.
They ripen in her full beam.

Suni, the young leaves under the vine
are wet in the moon; are they not forsaken?

SIN SŎK-CH'O (1909–), given name, Ŭng-sik, a journalist, has published poetry and criticism since 1935. He has two volumes of collected poems (1946 and 1959).

Sin Sŏk-ch'o

RAINSTORM

Spring is half over.
I am alone awake
and lie down in a room
deep in the mountains.

The rain and the wind
I hear around my pillow
shake the whole flower-bush
in the garden at the back.

Why are they so strong
when flowers bloom?

Time is so transient
it shakes all in passing.

PAK TU-JIN (1916–) had first appeared in the *Munjang* in 1939, and became one of the "Green Deer" group of poets, dealing mostly with nature, who came to prominence after 1945. His books of poetry include *The Sun* (1949), *Selected Poems* (1956), and *The White Wings* (1967). He won the Asia Foundation's Free Literature Prize in 1956.

Pak Tu-jin

HYMN TO GRAVEYARD

In the graveyard with rich golden lawn,
the round tombs are not lonely.

The white skulls may be shining in darkness.
Those bodies may smell fragrant too.

Died of sorrow they are not sad; they may long
only for the sun to shine brightly in the soil.

Red flowers in the golden grass, mountain birds.
The bodies rest in the warm May graves.

[1939]

Pak Tu-jin

DOVE

O dove, dove. Your eyes are pretty. Feathers, red feet are pretty
indeed. Come down to the earth, from that blue high and
far sky. Come down here like the scattering petals, all the
sky being hazy.

Trees, the trees with young leaves where you will sit are waiting.
Children are waiting. They are waiting for you in the green
lawn. Having scattered the green beans to feed you when you
come, children are waiting in the green lawn.

Coo-coo, dove. The roofs of the straw-thatched cottages, tile-roofed
houses, and of the Western-style houses; the roofs where you
will come and play are waiting. The yards where you will enjoy
are waiting.

Come to the sea too, to the mountains too. Flapping your white
wings, come to the village like petals. Coo-coo, dove. When
you coo, children come out. When you coo, new leaves sprout.
When you coo, flower-buds come up.

O dove, dove. Come down to everybody's shoulders, to the bloody
streets, to the tear-wet villages, like the falling petals, hazily
from far. With pretty eyes, pretty feathers, pretty red feet,
oh dove, come down. Coo-coo, dove, come down here.

Pak Tu-jin

A JAR

The belly of a jar,
full with blueness
drawn from the deep sky-well.
Warm sunshine passes through
sucking the jar's lips.
The pride of its
properly big belly.
Fragrant milk-flow,
flower-kneaded,
touching the breasts
swollen in longing
burned long.
O, give birth, birth to a child.
Pregnant with the sky,
a lump of the sun
drawn from the sky-well
and embraced.

CHO CHIHUN (1920–68), given name, Tong-t'ak, had along with his further study at Hehwa College (now Tongguk University) a strong background of Buddhism, the philosophy characterizing his poetic sensibility. He is credited with representing stillness especially in early works of nature poetry, which first appeared in the *Munjang*, an important literary monthly published in 1939–41, and later in *Green Deer Anthology* (1946) with two other co-authors. He published three volumes of his own poetry, including *Trailing Note* (1964), three books of essays, and a book of study on the history of Korean culture.

Cho Chihun

A NUN'S DANCE

A white wimple of thin gauze;
folded gracefully, butterfly.

Bluish head, close-cropped,
is veiled in the gossamer wimple.

Flowing light on the cheeks
is as beautiful as is sad.

Dark hours; quiet candles melt on an empty stand.
The moon sets in each leaf of paulownia.

The longer sleeves, the wider sky; flying, turning;
cotton anklets lovely as cucumber seeds, lightly up.

Rising gently, the black eyes gather
distant skies in a single starlight.

In the dappling globes of peach-blossomed face,
agonies twinkle despite life's pain.

Hands, bending, winding, folding again extending,
seem to be solemn worship in the depth of mind.

Midnight with crickets chirping nightlong;
white gossamer wimple, butterfly gracefully folded.

[1939]

Cho Chihun

AN OLD TEMPLE

Growing drowsy in beating
the temple's wooden drum,
a handsome youthful monk
has fallen asleep.

The Buddha smiles
in silence.

To the West Land,
hundreds of miles.

Peonies are falling
under the dazzling twilight.

[1941]

Cho Chihun

FALLING BLOSSOMS

No blaming the breeze
if blossoms fall.

Sparse stars beyond the screen
one by one turn unseen.

As a cuckoo sings
far hills draw near.

Why blow out the candle
while petals fall?

Scattering shadows,
flickering over the garden,

dimly redden
the white paper-doors.

With a fear
someone may notice

the pure heart
of a hermit,

I cannot help weeping
in the flower-falling dawn.

[1943]

PAK MOGWŎL (1917–), given name, Yŏng-jong, had written juvenile literature before his poetry appeared in the *Munjang* in 1939. He became known as one of the three "Green Deer" poets when their anthology was published in 1946. His publications include poetry, miscellaneous essays, anthologies, and criticism. He won the Asia Foundation's Free Literature Prize in 1955, and published *Orchid and Other Poems* (1959), and *Fine and Cloudy* (1964).

Pak Mogwŏl

A TRAVELLER

A traveller moves as the moon
moves through the clouds,

along the path in the wheat-field
across the ferry.

A simple line due south,
a hundred miles.

The evening dusk burns
over the brewing villages.

A traveller moves as the moon
moves through the clouds.

Pak Mogwŏl

IN MAY

Pine flower's pollen
scatters on a lone peak.

Warbles for the long day
in the month of May.

A house-bound maid
in a forest keeper's cottage
eavesdrops on the bird songs
leaning against the doorpost.

Pak Mogwŏl

AUTUMN

The train arrived late
at the country station,
and a flower-palankeen
was alone to wait
— yes, for the bride.
She will be coming
in a rose-pink skirt,
her cheeks rouged.
Autumnal breeze
at the country station,
a palankeen alone
was waiting there.

PAK NAM-SU (1913–) studied law at Chūō University, Tokyo, and his poetry first appeared in the *Munjang* magazine in 1940. He came from the North after the end of World War II. His publications include *A Hand-lantern* (1940), *Sketch of the Sea Gulls* (1958), and *God's Garbage* (1964).

Pak Nam-su

HANDS

The parting should not have been that way.
I should have held his hand with two
and cried or done something else.
Certainly I should have, and he should too.

But I did not stretch my hand out,
neither could he do so at all.
It would be happy for both of us
if we had parted quite otherwise.

He was more intimate than before,
and yet there was not one thing we could do.
I only looked down at my shameful hands.

It happened that his hands were left behind
in the field to save the fatherland,
he had no hand to offer, no hand.

Pak Nam-su

DURATION

Come to the windy side. No need
to pull her by the sleeve
with such fearful eyes.
She comes to you.

For your sake
she was conceived and grown.
And today, standing before you,
she is becoming big with child.

Greet her with a flowing thing
such as a smile. In fact,
she is with you.

Even after you leave
she remains like an eternity
in the space of purity.

KIM HYŎN-SŬNG (1913–) first published poetry while he was studying at Sungsil College in Pyongyang. He published *Selected Poems* in 1957.

Kim Hyŏn-sŭng

PLANE TREE

When I ask you if you have a dream,
plane tree,
your head suddenly gets wet in the sky-stream.

For yearning you never fade,
plane tree,
but with yourself you spread the shade.

When I come a long way,
alone and lonely,
plane tree,
you walk with me along the same way.

I wish I could lay my mind
deep in your root before leaving,
plane tree,
but I am not Almighty, nor can you be.

Is there a rich earth to greet you afar?
I only long to watch you as your neighbor,
plane tree,
where my familiar windows keep open to the star.

KIM YONG-HO (1912–), a college teacher, poet, and anthologist, was once a student of law at Meiji University, Tokyo. He published a few books of poetry such as *Pageant* (1941) and *Wings* (1956), and wrote an epic, *Glory of the Southern Sea*, dealing with Admiral Yi Sun-sin. He has edited and compiled numerous volumes of anthologies of contemporary Korean poetry.

Kim Yong-ho

WINGS (II)

I've climbed the ladder step by step with care,
am now at the top having attained my majority.
Mother,
where shall I go from here?

Still far too encumbered with craving
to remain one with that distant air;
and too late to go down —
the rungs were removed by time.

Thoughtless children clap their hands
at my hapless stunts.
And I hear
someone shouting
you Pierrot
Pierrot.

Mother, tell me,
why didn't you give me
wings for flying?

[From *Wings*, 1956]

Kim Yong-ho

WINGS (III)

Space, an endless distance.

A signal blinks at the intersecting thoughts,
and a sweet touch is pregnant with colors.

Time revolves on the circling orbit, while
Mona Lisa smiles en route to primitive ages.

A typewriter calculates the numbers.

The day when nature ascends and man descends,
here the wings become a flag and it flutters.

Round a spot, composing a circle,
here the wings become waves, and billow.

[From *Wings*, 1956]

CHANG SŎ-ŎN (1912–), a graduate of Yŏnhŭi College, now Yŏnse University, was once involved in drama too, and started publishing his modernistic poems in the 1930s. His *Collected Poems* was published in 1959.

Chang Sŏ-ŏn

AN OLD VASE

An ancient ceramic.
Sloping shoulders, like tears.
No arms.

Frozen pale.
A lonesome urn
like an old nurse.

The obtuse lips are full
of unseasonable grasses.
And inside, a quarter of water,
having forgotten the color of sky,
dreams of valleys.

Dusk's blue shadow,
spread with the fallen petals,
plods backward across the window
as if riding a tortoise.

Then it emits again
light fragrance.

[From *New Poets*, 1940]

YANG MYŎNG-MUN (1913–) studied law in Senshū University, Tokyo, while writing poetry there. He came from Pyongyang to Seoul after 1945, and published four volumes of poetry, including *Martian* (1955), *Blue Legend* (1959), and *Selected Poems* (1965).

Yang Myŏng-mun

STONE IMAGE OF BUDDHA

Flute tunes
from far antiquity
with delicacy
drift about your mouth.

Muffled music,
  abstruse and profound,
swirls around
the lotus-seat.

Merciful
figure
superior
to life and death.

O those eyelids
of yours!
Moved to tears
in ecstasies.

KIM CHONG-HAN (1916–44), pen name, Ŭlp'aso, first appeared in the *Munjang* in 1939, and he was said to be "capable of holding sadness skillfully with wit."

Kim Chong-han

A LANDSCAPE WITH AN OLD WELL

A weeping willow stands by an old well,
in which snatches of the May sky fell.

— Young lady,
is that the same cuckoo that was singing there last year?
You, a quiet lady, smile like a gourd flower.

And you draw up the blue sky flowing over the bucket,
draw up the blue legends flowing over the bucket.

The bellow of a bull, again flowing, comes in across the heights,
and from the water jar also overflow your blue skies.

HAM HYŎNG-SU (1916–?), a graduate of Hehwa College, began publishing his poems in the thirties.

Ham Hyŏng-su

A SUNFLOWER EPITAPH

Do not set up a cold stone before my tomb.
Instead, do plant those yellow sunflowers round it,
and have an endless barley-field show their long stems.
May the yellow sunflower be regarded as my splendid love, longing
    ever for the sun.
When a lark shoots at the sky from the green field, may it be
    taken as my dream, still flying up.

YI HO-U (1912–), a journalist and *sijo* writer, published a volume of the *sijo* in 1955. Also, he has a book of study in old *sijo* poetry.

Yi Ho-u

THE SUN SETTING RIVER
(*sijo*)

The setting sun burns over the river,
 and a boat flows through.
The far village dinner smoke
 suffuses the bamboo bush.
There where the blue hill ends
 a snowy egret stands.

YUN TONG-JU (1917–45), born in Manchuria, studied English at Dōshisha University, Kyoto, and was arrested by the Japanese police on his way home from Japan. He died in Hukuoka (Fukuoka) Prison a few months before the end of World War II. His posthumous book of verse, *The Sky and the Wind and Poetry*, was published in 1955.

Yun Tong-ju

ANOTHER HOME

Tonight when I am back home
my skeleton has followed me to my bed.

The dark room is open to the universe
and wind blows down as if from heaven.

Looking in my bones that weather
nicely in the dark, something weeps.
Is it myself
or the bones,
or the lovely soul?

A faithful dog
barks at darkness all night.

He must be, in fact,
trying to drive me away.

Yes, I must leave
like a hunted man,
I will go to another beautiful home
unnoticed to my skeleton.

[1941]   [1955]

Section II

Younger Voices
Since August 1945

KO TU-DONG (1903–), pen name, Hwangsan, has been writing *sijo* poetry and criticism of it since the late 1920s. He founded a *sijo* magazine in 1953.

Ko Tu-dong

STAR
(sijo)

There is a star that has turned
away from this immense universe.

The sounds of water and the wind
arise friendly, circling the star.

Its mind, as firm as stone,
is moistened with the orchid fragrance.

YI HYO-SANG (1905–), pen name, Hansol, a graduate of Tokyo University with a major in German, is presently chairman of the National Assembly. He has published five volumes of poetry, including *My Land* (1966).

Yi Hyo-sang

DAHLIA

A dahlia, standing on an O,
the central point in my garden;

a dahlia has light which
radiates like the sun,

and the centripetal force
to draw the eyes and mind;

a dahlia, after all,
living on the green dream.

YI KYŎNG-SUN (1905–), pen name, Tonggi, a graduate of a dental college in Japan, is now a principal of a junior high school in Kyŏngnam. He published three books of verse, including *Ode on Life* (1951).

Yi Kyŏng-sun

ROMANCE

1

In the beautiful cobalt sky
a warbler and a white snake
went into the cloud making an S.

2

The orange patterned sea
is wet with a full moon.
An anchovy is exiled after kissing
shellfish's lips giving tongue to her.

3

On the table of a nihilist
who eats the dusk with gusto,
the shellfish with the anchovy's
posthumous child lay down.
But, from the cloud, no news
of the warbler soothing her snake.

PAK KI-WŎN (1908–), a journalist, attended Nippon University, Tokyo. He published a book of verse, *Cold Fire* in 1953, together with Ch'oe Chae-hyŏng.

Pak Ki-wŏn

CLOUD

Shouldn't imagine a bloody painting.
It is weight itself like the wind.

A shower has just passed
deep mountain recesses.

The mountainous clouds,
cotton flowers up in the air.

Suddenly hangs, at ease,
a bridge of the rainbow.

Far on the bridge, someone opens
the heavenly gate to see a parade off.

Who is that
nice looking lady?

KIM YONG-JE (1909–) studied at Chūō University, Tokyo, and participated actively in the proletarian poetry movement in Japan for some time until he was put in prison. He published five volumes of Japanese poetry before 1945, and since then he has been writing both poetry and prose in Korean. His first book of Korean poems, *The Mountain, Heartless*, came out in 1954.

Kim Yong-je

A MOUNTAIN RETREAT

Way out of noisy Seoul,
here in a mountain retreat by myself.
When the vacant wind makes me long for people,
the white clouds bring past romance to bloom.

The bedside folding screen
does not have to be an artist's work.
Open any window, a landscape is there,
flatteringly moving my senses.

If a wedding dress, say, was to be taken off,
it would have been better without, from the first.
A candle is to be put out anyway —
What's wrong with the half moon in a daydream?

Sweetness alone would not do
much with the fruits of life.
In a jar of small persimmons, sour and rough,
new wine is brewing up as I hear the sound.

CHŎNG HUN (1911–), a teacher and leader of a literary group in Ch'ung-nam Province, writes with much local flavor. He has published the *Mŏdŭllyŏng Hill* (1948) and three other books of poetry and the *sijo*.

Chŏng Hun

DRUNKEN NIGHT

The sunset. I wish I could break my heart
and throw my whole body away.

Drink is surely better than man.
Not a single guy can rule over me
when my body burns up.

Powerful drunkenness, even dignified
more than indignation —
I give a good command to those mice.

Not that I grumble at the betrayers,
or rebel against my natural misfortune,
I just howl out towards the emptiness
of the extensive heavens.

I wonder, am I wine
or wine is me? It doesn't matter.
I am proud of being a giant.

How come the sky is so low
as choking me? Besides,
the earth is swinging. That's nice.

YI SŎLCHU (1908–), given name, Yong-su, was put in prison by the Japanese while studying at Nippon University, Tokyo, and later wandered through Manchuria and China until the liberation in 1945. He published nine volumes of verse including *The Gleanings of Life* (1957).

Yi Sŏlchu

AT A CREMATORIUM

Those who do not want to return to life,
who are afraid of coming to life again . . .

Their bodies are by no means revivable,
and are to burn for double death.

May the soul, if any, also die.
You have had enough trouble.

The smoke of oblivion over the abode of shades.
What will be left in time and space, all empty?

Those who are afraid of coming back to life
lie down here side by side.

SŎL CHŎNG-SIK (1912–53) attended Meiji University, Tokyo, and had also studied in the United States. He had worked for the United States Military Government in South Korea before he went to the North, where he served as an interpreter at the Panmunjom conferences for some time. Later he was executed by the communists. He wrote poetry since the 1930s and published two volumes in Seoul, *Bell* (1947), and *Grape* (1948).

Sŏl Chŏng-sik

GRAPE

For how many remains
are these sacrifices offered
way up on the hill in full?

Fruit as it is, soft and nice —
say, like my baby's head,
but it has wisdom
to turn to salt within a night
for single teeth that may
pickle a sin for nine generations.

The grape
trembles dangerously
between flesh and soul.

YI T'AE-GŬK (1913–), pen name, Wŏlha or Tongmang, attended Waseda, Tokyo, and later graduated from Seoul University. He is now teaching Korean literature at Ewha Women's University. He published a few books and articles on the *sijo* besides his own *sijo* poetry.

Yi T'ae-gŭk

MARCH
(sijo)

Azaleas, with buds swelling,
   restless, stretching in the hill.
No more snow, which was once deep,
   and the rabbits are asleep.
March is mother's mind,
   her warm heart, all warmer.

CH'OE CHAE-HYŎNG (1914–), a graduate of Komazawa University, Japan, published a book of verse, *Cold Fire* (1953), together with Pak Ki-wŏn.

Ch'oe Chae-hyŏng

A PLASTER BUST

With lips firmly closed
it dare not say anything as it has

known the wordy, lousy whispers
coming from dirty blood;

and suffered from the blizzard
of time striking the window;

and nobody to love any more,
no more life desirable.

No longer sad, it has closed all
as peacefully as looking cold.

KIM SU-DON (1915–67), a product of the *Munjang*, studied at Nippon University, Tokyo. He published two books of sad and sensuous poetry, *Calling Swallow* (1947) and *A Melancholy Emperor* (1953).

Kim Su-don

A MELANCHOLY EMPEROR

Lighting a candle
in the bright day . . .
that's of no use.

Colorless song.

Anemone is a sweet love,
melancholy lady in thick purple.

The clouds and poetry and dream.
This feast makes me lose my appetite.

I enjoy a secret habit of drinking
without knowing how long.

The war comes into the consciousness
of a world severed from knowledge and reason.
Too many heroes.

Shall I become a wandering emperor
on a desolate island in the distant sea?

CHANG SU-CH'ŎL (1916–) came from North Korea in 1950, and writes poetry for children also. He published two books of verse, *Village of Lyricism* (1960), and *Wandering* (1966).

Chang Su-ch'ŏl

LONGING

Evening dusk wet in mist
was lonely at the window.

In this twilight the writhing flowers
dressed in solitude were blooming.

I would rather have been an idiot:
perhaps I was already.

I could not see you at all
through a screen of yearning for you.

When I rolled my eyes
a fountain seemed to clean the stars.

You were going far away like the mist
through the stars in which we used to swim.

Unable to call you back
at the window, with nothing I could do,

I only waved my hands over again
counting uselessly sad years.

At the end of slender fingers
misty evening dusk sat alone.

HAM YUN-SU (1916–), a graduate of Nippon University, Tokyo, first appeared in the *Maek* magazine in 1938. He came from the North to Seoul during the Korean War, and published four volumes of poetry, including *Parrot* (1939), *Musk Cat* (1958), and *Selected Poems* (1965).

Ham Yun-su

FLOWER-SNAKE

Smile spreads over the lips with opium.
Eyes shine only in darkness like an owl.

Flowery-snake, whirling around pillow
like an immortal ghost,
enchants me into a mirage.
Close your poisonous mushroom lips.

With body odors, bewitching smell,
snake holds a huge feast of Hell
in the mystic grave.

Countless coiled feelers on the breast.
The cursed belly cannot conceive.

SŎL CH'ANG-SU (1916–), pen name, P'asŏng, studied at Nippon University, Tokyo. He has published a book of poetry and a few plays. Formerly a member of the National Assembly, now the president of a local newspaper, he has led the cultural development of his home province, Kyŏngnam, through the arts festivals and literary-circle activities.

Sŏl Ch'ang-su

AN OLD HAWK
(at the foot of the Mt. Halla)

I am not primarily a bird of contemplation,
but of thorough will and action.
My nature has nothing to do
with an owl's cowardice,
crows' forming a flock,
nor with a fox's cunning; yet I
never surrender to hunger and solitude.

Look at
my eyes, beak, wings,
talons and breast, all supported
by a full fighting spirit,
which is not haughty fierceness.
I hate aristocracy.
Only because of fastidiousness
I do not eat carrion.

Alone at the seashore, I blankly
watch the sunset over the western sea
with remorse, late in life,
for having ignored my gift.
My youth has gone
with the rocks, wind and sky
apart from the mountains' prosperity,
and I pray only for the coming generations.

Now I will flap my wings
to fly to you,
my everlasting homeland.
Mountains,
assure this prayer of mine.

YI SANG-NO (1916–), a journalist and magazine editor, published three volumes of poetry, *Way Home* (1953), *Improper Lyricism* (1957), and *With Time* (1961), besides some prose. He is now working for the *Tonga Ilbo*.

Yi Sang-no

IN THE STARLIGHT

Starlight travelling forever
makes eyes look up at flower.

Quiet but warm words I hear
from the flitting clean images.

My home . . . people were close
many happy years ago.

In the everflowing starlight
flowers bloom and bear fruits.

Shines afresh a mystery of life
among the leaves coming back in love.

CHO HYANG (1917–), given name, Sŏp-che, was a leading member of the Latter-Half Period group of avant-garde poets in the fifties. He is most conscious of the theories and techniques of Western modernism, and has proved himself to be one of the best among the postwar Korean "modernists." He also published a novel in 1953.

Cho Hyang

AN EPISODE

With bloodshot eyes and firm lips, the boy calmly aimed at the
    hand.
The girl's palm perched, lightly like a butterfly, on the end of
    his rifle.
From the muzzle of the rifle, a column of blue smoke was puffed
    up.
She looked out at the sea through the hole in her pierced palm.

— Hey, how could the sea be round like this?

The terrified sea gulls were driving their heads in the desolate
    hillside, one after another, and were fossilizing themselves
    in white.

Cho Hyang

ESQUISSE

1

Closing her eyes
Suna gropes for my hands.
I put mine on hers gently.
Warm.
— That's the way it is.
— What's that?
— Life.
Suna's brow is white, wide.

2

There is my lost lake
in the eyes
of Suna.
A swan crosses
the mountains of my old days.

3

Slenderly,
the age of twenty-five sighs.
— I've grown a year older!
Suna again closes her eyes.
— That's the way it is.
White gloom spreads on her forehead.

4

— Oh, I'm only in my petticoat.
— Shall I turn my back?
— Please.
On my brow I feel the cold sky over the window.
"Rustle of a woman undressing far away."
— All right now.

5

Suna puts make-up on.
— Make-up is art, isn't it?
My face projects over Suna's shoulder.
There, the two faces get together in the mirror.
— Just like a father and his daughter.

6

A necklace on Suna's white neck.
A pretty yellow key is hung on it.
— I'll try to unlock your secret with this key.

7

Becoming intoxicated with the voice of Stefano,
I touch Suna, with my eyes . . . for a long time.
— Why do you stare at me like that?
— Because you are beautiful.
— That's the way it is.

8

I part from my Suna.
The black night street.
The things
that jump at the windshield of a taxi;
something like sleet, like butterflies;
the fragments of my unrealities.
I catch them in my breast.
Suna's eyes, so many,
sown in the black sky.
Twinkle.
        "That's the way it is."

Cho Hyang

NIGHT OF THE EARTH, ONE DAY

A perfectly white hand has fallen
    on the black base of night.
The last elevator going down. The masquers
    carrying out the cast bandages.
A boy's whistle, detained in a microfilm.
    White. E string.
The weather in which the cactuses come up
    from women's bodies. Spitting sounds
        outside the earth.
A line of the black images without necks
    across a swamp area.
Here, the dialogues of cryptogam
    notably hung out.
Long, long past myself is identifiable
    with a dropped name-card.
Swaying politicians like corn.
    Anemic rush hours.
A group of the Presidents who have prepared
    fireworks for a future funeral
        is caught in a shower
            before the gate of the opera house.
A vision of the white, long fingers
    checking a euthanasia
        on a white hemp-cloth bed.
        Çà et là.
Hey — ! Hey — ! No Sara.
    Nobody is there, really.

YI IN-SŎK (1917–), a journalist, came from the North to South Korea in 1948, and published two volumes of poetry, *Love* (1955), and *Paper House and the Sky* (1961). He won the Free Literature Association Award in 1959.

Yi In-sŏk

BUTTERFLIES

Yellow butterflies. They were flying
in an oppressive silence
before and behind me.

From their dazzling color
a sound like a stream or wind
was flowing out.

Certainly it was a sob
flowing down from a remote place
to the nearest core of me.

With the cry
the butterflies turned to a vision
or returned to past dreams.

It was my old memory circling in and out
that was waving ahead and behind,
a mirror beyond my reach or possession.

KIM KYŎNG-NIN (1918–) studied at the College of Engineering, Waseda University, and participated in VOU, a modernist group in Japan. After 1945 he became a member-contributor of the *Sin Siron* magazine and a member of the Latter-Half Period group. His poetry was anthologized in *A New City and the Citizens' Chorus* (1949) and *The Modern Temperature* (1957).

Kim Kyŏng-nin

SEOUL WHERE THE SUN FALLS AT A RIGHT ANGLE

The sun falls into the streets of Seoul
at a right angle,
where the plane trees are so green
I fear they may dye my heart.

What did the army trucks
ever bring to me indeed,
running at full speed
over my lonely image?

"Do you know my days past,
you who pass through
pushing aside the nets like a pigeon?"
And
"can you guarantee
any future for my friends and for me?"

Standing on the Moment
where the brilliant images
once so deeply annoyed me,
never can be renewed,
I weary much
of conversation with such
as a professor in the afternoon.
Then an argument passes by soon
touching my skin like the wind.

No one may understand
the sadness of a fragment
of a face broken on the pavement.

I wave the thinking leaf
bleached like a handkerchief,
and turn the street corner
where the twilight rises higher
like a telephone pole,
and I try to breathe the green
of a plane tree after all.

HAN HA-UN (1919–) has been writing bitter poems about lepers since he became a victim himself after he had graduated from Peking University. He published four books of verse, *Selected Poems* (1948), *Grass Whistle* (1955), two *Collected Poems* (1956 and 1964), and an autobiography, *Lonely Life* (1958).

Han Ha-un

PUNISHMENT

Charged with being a leper . . .
This is a punishment I cannot understand.

I have no way to defend myself.
What law is there that I could cite?

From old times, I know, a human crime
has been to be punished by man.

But me — why should I be forced to keep away
in this desolate air? Please, why is it?

Charged with being a leper . . .
This is a punishment I cannot understand.

HWANG KŬM-CH'AN (1919–) came from North Korea in 1946 and has published poetry in *Ch'ŏngp'odo, Munye,* and *Hyŏndae Munhak.* His first book of poetry, *The Here and Now,* came out in 1965.

Hwang Kŭm-ch'an

DOOR

Declining hours.
The rain falls to the cold streets.

All the doors are locked
before the way of my fated existence.

On this spot,
inevitably tense to me,
struggling I knock on a door.

But the door remains closed, and instead
numerous wounds nail up my heart.
It seems too spiteful.

Now I think: man is doomed to vanish
after knocking on doors hopelessly
over and over all his life.

His blood, if it blooms, is but a reed.
Its flower fades in lamenting wind.
Then purple, empty air is left in silence.

Those who have left after crying
in front of this door, in the rain,
for the last thousand years . . .
I, too, am striking a door right here.

KIM CHONG-MUN (1919–), a graduate of Athènes Français in Tokyo and formerly brigadier general of the South Korean Army, published five books of poetry, including *Human Formation* (1958) and *New Poems* (1965). He won the first Free Literature Association Award.

Kim Chong-mun

RESISTANCE IN JUNE

It was June, it was warm June.

I was born of the incarnation
of a squarish resistance.

I had to keep a small hut
at the foot of a certain barren mountain,
looking at a rifle like myself,
a rifle produced by the heat of the earth.

Then what happened
the next day when Jesus Christ
was said to have been resurrected?
I had to live waiting for uneasy Saturdays.

And I always had to live
searching for the enemies
on my map, under the distant
blue skies.

Among the acacia trees, I had to live
smelling gunpowder which was thicker
than the lingering light of radium,
and like myself, like my body's odors.

I have had to live until now
still as an old soldier
to resist the countless "I"s,
someone like myself.

Kim Chong-mun

HUMAN FORMATION

Sunshine between the two weeks.
    At noon
    on Sunday
    he drinks wine thicker than sunshine.

Two faces,
    reflecting
    in the glass,
    combine into one
    and again separate.
    The glass occupies space.

Drinking space,
    the man is a spatial-
    alcoholic,
    lain long between the two weeks.

The past Saturday:
    do not grasp him.
    The coming Monday:
    do not draw him.
    Sunshine is today's.

Nothing is seen by him who has become
    space. His inside
    becomes home for the legends
    of all weekdays to ruin themselves.

Already
    memories
    and hopes
    dissolve into space;
    and its crystal, the rose blooms.

Kim Chong-mun

CACTI

The sands were falling down from the sky.
Men were making the plain and hills,
shouting in the wind
like a thinking sand.

Thinking of the thought of happiness,
they were living on the dead ruins, still
building houses and cultivating gardens.

Resigned to remaining in the desert,
they travelled, holding the skulls,
to look for an oasis.

Little blood
shed by the passing sun was seen,
like a sun in exile.

The sands were falling down from the sky.
A woman with face veiled in a black scarf
was going through the desert far away,
heaven and earth, all desert.

KU SANG (1919–), given name, Sang-jun, a Catholic poet from North Korea and graduate of Nippon University with a major in religion, published three books of verse, including *The Poetry of the Parched Ground*, and received the Seoul City Cultural Award for Literature in 1958. He also published a collection of criticism in social affairs.

Ku Sang

ENEMY'S GRAVES

O souls, lain asleep in lines,
would not have closed their eyes.

With our hands that pulled the trigger
against your hearts until yesterday in anger,
we have collected and buried
those rotten flesh and bones,
choosing a sunny hill, and also turfed.

Death is more generous
than hatred or love.

Here, the home lands
for the souls of yours and mine,
each borders the other within a few miles.

Absolute desolation all around
oppresses my heart in bonds.

Being alive, you were related to me
only with hostility;
now on the contrary, your resentment
that you could not vent
is changed to stay with my hope.

Through the spring sky so low
clouds casually flow
towards the North.

Hearing the guns from somewhere
I burst into tears before these
graves of regret and care.

NO YŎNG-NAN (1919– ?), a graduate of Tokyo Imperial Women's College and a modernistic poetess, published two books of poetry, *Splendid Co-ordinates* (1953), *Black Jewel* (1959), and a collection of short stories, *Last Feast* (1958).

No Yŏng-nan

A GIRL IN ME

A girl in me,
who assures my happiness with a bloody pen:
you are an eternal Pierrot knowing no death.

Even if the eyes of God, coming and leaving in secret, may refuse
    your beauty,
you are a star still staring at me, my window surrounded
    by darkness.

While my old faith is being dyed in a counter current of night,
my girl, you smile coldly like a flower of cold crystal in my sight.

Seeing you, my consciousness like a blue splinter in blood
has no power to lead you to death, even long after.
Conversations fluttering like the torn banners of a temporary
    theatre
on ruins made by burning life
hurt, moreover, your will to be alive.

Say the footsteps of God, passing by with a wink at one moment,
would refuse your delight, my girl,
you are still my everlasting star reviving even in sadness;
and a flowery defender justifying my clumsy existence.

When the smoke of civilization rushes dark into my organs,
and you stand in that solitary melody,
I notice clearly
your beautiful silence,
and your breaths wishing to live with me forever.

PAK HUNSAN (1919–), given name, Yu-sang, a journalist, studied law at Nippon University, Tokyo. He published a book of poetry, *The More As Time Passes* (1958).

Pak Hunsan

STANDING ON THE DARK

That indignation,
pierced deep enough to the heart.
Thunder.
Tear the sky into pieces once again
with a fire-sword, the blade of song!

Fire-balls,
seizing the darkness,
come through the depth of night.
The power,
your anger!
There opens future in black blue.

As I outstretch the breast
at night like this,
a clear way gets closer.

Like the compressed air,
like the angry air
running through an iron pipe
deep in a mine-gallery,
let us go over
breathless stairs one by one.

Roaring at the deadly night,
let us all hurry on
taking it away with us.

YI TONG-JU (1920–), a teacher, studied at Hehwa College (Tongguk University) and obtained recommendation in the *Munye* magazine in 1950. He published two books of poetry, *Wedding Night* and *Kang-gang Suwŏllae*, and was awarded the Korean Writers Association Prize in 1960, and the May Literary Prize in 1965.

Yi Tong-ju

KANG-GANG SUWŎLLAE
a folk dance

A shoal of fishes
rushing in a swirl.

Flowery hands make a circle,
the moon-ring turns round.

"Kang-gang suwŏllae" —
sentiment in high tone.

A peacock got drunk
in the white rose garden.

Jump. Jump. Let us jump.
Kang-gang suwŏllae.

Fathoms long hat-feathers whirl,
tapes twist around the grain stack.

Once permeate, the moonlight
is stronger than drink.

Banners are torn,
reeds fall down.

Kang-gang suwŏllae,
Kang-gang suwŏllae.

CHO YŎNGAM (1920–), given name, Sŭng-Wŏn, a graduate of Hehwa College, came from the North shortly before the Korean War. His publications include a book of war poetry, *Coming Through the Dead Bodies and Blood-Sea* (1951), novels, and other prose works.

Cho Yŏngam

NOTHINGNESS
Canto 5

I pointed at the white moon with a stick,
and Sami, a handsome boy did not know what it meant, he said.

The handsome boy, Sami, said he did not know
the white moon swam in every river.

This boy, Sami, did not know the simple law
that flowers bloom every spring, he said.

KIM SANG-OK (1920–), pen name, Ch'ojŏng, has been writing widely — poetry, the *sijo*, and poetry for children since 1938 when he appeared in the *Munjang*. His published books of poetry are *The Songs of My Old Haunts* (1949), *The Poetry of Heresy* (1949), *Dress* (1953), *The Songs of Trees and Stones* (1956), a collection of his *sijo*, *Grass-flute* (1947), and two volumes of juvenile poetry.

Kim Sang-ok

IN A CAVE

A sunflower, which has come out longing for a new sun nobody has seen, stands here as a guard, trailing its stamen.

In the dark cave where there is a position only, surrounded in many folds, and no direction, there rises a strange smell like sounding, like a sound.

On the countless skulls, flowers blow, and the countless skulls stand up, all holding the flowers like candles here and there.

Butterflies in a crowd that got used to the long darkness go back sightless. On their wings, left useless already, come up the minute diplopic eyeballs, dappling, needed again.

CHO PYŎNG-HWA (1921–) majored in physics and chemistry at Tokyo Teachers College, and has published more than ten volumes of poetry since 1945, beginning with *The Heritage I Want to Throw Away* (1949). He was awarded the Asia Foundation's Free Literature Prize in 1959.

Cho Pyŏng-hwa

FALLEN LEAVES LIVE TOGETHER

I live lying down on the fallen leaves.
Fallen leaves live together.
Let us forget about the past.
My ears are interested in the edge of the sky
where they hear the leaves fall in faint voices;
the thin skin is irritated as the sunshine falls.
I want to live for a place always unseen.
Where I approach, leaves fall down.
My body is already thrown among the dead leaves,
and I live on drinking a new sadness nearby.
I walk over the fallen leaves in the rainy night,
come back treading sadness in the rainy night.
My voice makes the night cold,
and I sit up all night rubbing my voice.
Fallen leaves live together.
I live lying down on the fallen leaves,
live for an unseen place drinking sadness.

Cho Pyŏng-hwa

AT A WEDDING CEREMONY

Women with red lips above long necks
are set forth like merchandise
under the banners.

Men with closed pig-like lips,
heads drooped, like sun-fearing animals,
watch the women.

The wedding couple thinks of tonight's manners,
and the honored guests proudly think of
offering long congratulations.

For the bride brighter than Cleopatra
and the bridegroom uneasy in his large shirt,
the red lipped
and the pig-lipped
decently pin on their breasts
paper-flowers instead of iron medals.

A so-called poet
reads a useless poem.

I no longer have anything to long for, but wish
I could hear something from Latin America
through the banners,
sitting by the children who drop cake crumbs.

KIM SU-YŎNG (1921–68) studied at Yŏnhŭi College and was engaged in theatre until 1945. He published a book of poetry, *Play of the Moon-land* (1959), and has appeared in many anthologies.

Kim Su-yŏng

SNOW

Snow is alive.
Snow fallen is alive.
Snow fallen to the ground is alive.

Let us cough,
young poet, let us cough.
Let us cough against the snow.
Let us do so without anxiety
so that the snow may see.

Snow is alive.
For the soul and flesh
that forgot about death, let us cough.
Snow is alive until the morning dawns.

Let us cough,
young poet, let us cough.
Looking at the snow
let us spit out the phlegm right now,
which stuck to the heart all night.

Kim Su-yŏng

THE WORDS OF A CERTAIN POET

The words of a certain poet
who was in envy of a skylark, saying
it is free and controls the blue sky,
must be corrected.

One who has ever flown high
for freedom surely knows:
for what a skylark sings,
why freedom smells bloody,
why a revolution is lonely;

and why a revolution
has to be lonely.

Kim Su-yŏng

WITH FLIES

To me, frail in health,
the flies are no longer the same.

Civilization which should have abolished
its task long ago annoys me this much.

Along with the cold autumn wind,
tradition
has barely settled down somewhere
in the shadows of trees like the birds.

Why I am concerned with my sickness,
why I hang on my sickness may be
because I am still healthy,
because I am a man of great sorrow,
because I am a man of great composure,

may be because I know how to die
like the sound of a quiet fly
shining in a vast sunny place.

PAK T'AE-JIN (1921–) studied English at Rikkyō University, Tokyo, and spent four years in England working for a Korean business firm. His poems were anthologized in *The Modern Temperature* and in other collections. His book of poetry is *Transfiguration*.

Pak T'ae-jin

A SLANT WAY

The ceaseless wind moves about on a slant way.
The afternoon throws a clear shade on different worlds.
The traces of a forsaken youth are far over the ridge,
and I choose to neglect a prepared elegy.

Are my eyes carelessly cast on this way,
where forgetfulness seems to flow again
when I am perhaps conscious of the eyes of Narcissus?
Loneliness, trying not to be abandoned by time.

A shadow lying nowhere is going,
like the shadow in which the afternoon clearly settled,
along the way where some remains incline side by side.

YI HAN-JIK (1921–), pen name, Moknam, made his early debut through the *Munjang* in 1939 before going to Keiō University, Tokyo. He published *Poison*, a book of poetry. In 1955 he founded a short-lived monthly in Seoul, the *Chŏnmang*. He is now living in Tokyo.

Yi Han-jik

ON THE MARGIN

Should I walk all the way through
just like this?

Rubbing the strangers' shoulders
I go along the street in Pusan,
and must stop.

What kind of feeling is this
pouring suddenly like a shower
on a man of thirty-three
who can't even be sad any more?

The watch stopped long ago.
Touching it in my pocket,
I in the tenderest mood
look in at a flower shop.

Crimson of gladioli penetrates
through my body, becoming dizzy,
and flies out over infinity.

I, motionless, shut my eyes.
The midsummer's sun is hot.
Someone whispers in my ear.

"Rien, rien."
The whisper repeats
in a persuasive voice.

Rien. Rien.

YI YŎNG-SUN (1921–), formerly a high military officer, studied economics at Tokyo University. He published three volumes of verse, including *The Third Chaos* (1958), and a few pieces of fiction.

Yi Yŏng-sun

THE MAIL OF DEATH

The blue wings of dusk are coming down
to an empty, old battle field, arms thrown.

Back on the silent gun-platform, between the stones,
crickets chirrup alone, not forgetting the season.

An armful of military mail from somewhere
has arrived here like the word of pigeons.

Where have those who would be glad gone?
Not all died, yet nobody is receiving the mail.

Only a young sentry under a pine tree, in the dark,
on the withered grass, watches the barbed wire.

Bowwow, a dog barks far away —
Whose death is it calling?

KIM CHONG-SAM (1922–) was engaged in theater for some time after he had studied at Bunka Gakuin, Tokyo. He was anthologized in *The War and Music and Hope* (1957).

Kim Chong-sam

TWELVE TONE STAIRS

The face covered with a plaster,
a dark daytime.
Angle of the clouds
moving more in a drought.
My market for an ephemeral crowd.
Sartre's lavatory smoking thick.
Made-up show-windows of manikins
found innocent just before death.
A still birth.
Silent perfection.

KIM CH'UN-SU (1922–), a college teacher, poet, and critic, studied the fine arts at Nippon University, Tokyo, and published a few volumes of poetry including *Flag, The Clouds and Roses, The Death of a Girl in Budapest* (1959), and *Flower Sketches* (1959), in addition to *Formal Study of Korean Poetry* (1958). Both the Korean Poets Association and the Asia Foundation offered him literary awards.

Kim Ch'un-su

PRELUDE FOR A FLOWER

I now am a dangerous animal.
The touch of my hands makes you
an unknown, remote darkness.

On the end of a branch
of an existence, you bloom
and fall without a name.

I cry all night having lit a wick
of memory in this nameless darkness
sunken in my eyelids.

My cry will gradually become
a night whirlwind shaking a tower,
and then gold, having pierced stone.

. . . Veiled bride of mine . . .

Kim Ch'un-su

FLOWER

It had been
no more than a sign
until I chose to name it.

And when I did so
it came to me
and became a flower.

Will anyone call me by name
fit for my scent and color
as I did the flower?
I want to come to her or him
as that person's flower.

We all wish
to become something:
an unforgettable meaning,
you to me, and I to you.

Kim Ch'un-su

THE WALL

The wall comes near.
An old pagoda-tree comes near.
A headless doll too.
(Where are they coming from?)

The bronze clock on the wall
in Notre Dame's corridor
strikes one at night.
Somewhere, on the bottom of a swamp,
a leech cries.
The red, red flowers fall
and are piled on his tears.

KIM KU-YONG (1922–), a graduate of Sŏnggyun'gwan University, was awarded the New Writers' Prize for his poetry in 1956. He also translated a few Chinese classics into Korean.

Kim Ku-yong

SWALLOW

Ten, hundred, thousand . . . swallows are crossing this fiord-fear over the forlorn sea, dreaming of a lovely land. My dizziness can be a fate like the corpse of a swallow floating up and down on a certain ocean. But the swallows are flying over the rolled up billows, leaving no room for even a rose or tree or eaves-nest. Let's say, that is the power with which my swallow flies on the abstract bottom required by an unrequited effort.

YU CHŎNG (1922–), a journalist, studied philosophy at Jōchi (Sophia) University, Tokyo, and was given individual guidance by the Japanese poet, Horiguchi Daigaku, while writing poetry in Japanese. He later came from the North to Seoul in 1946, and published a book of Korean verse, *The Poetry of Love and Hatred* (1957). He edited, with Yi Pong-nae, *Korean Poetry, Vol. 1* (1955).

Yu Chŏng

LAMP POEM

The window used to be light every evening,
now today as I see it again
neither a lamp nor your face shows there,
but the dark dusk settled in like its home.
I feel a chill as if I have seen blood.
Let me light a lamp,
that warm stuff.
When my breath — gloom goes down
through the icy lamp chimney,
the oil smell condenses around its valley.
In the grayish fog
your faint back flickers,
going in tears by yourself.
They say, the war has taken you.
What is that dim way I cannot go along?
Like fog,
my dear one fades showing only her back.
A lamp, burning cold.
My shadow, shaking coldly, is left alone
at the black window as another night comes.

CHŎNG HAN-MO (1923–), a graduate of Seoul University where he teaches modern Korean literature, published three books of poetry including *Superfluity of Chaos*. He also has a book of study in modern Korean fiction.

Chŏng Han-mo

FADE TO ENTER

A naked image of poplar
comes in to my quiet sight
in an orderly movement,
moving as a day
silently sets into stone.
No wind shakes
the gathering distant view.

At the end of its trunk
which has thrown all achievements
and bright colors down,
the last branch fades far away
and becomes the sky.

Chŏng Han-mo

EXPRESSION

When grief stagnates
in the clear eyes,
you look down without sighs.

When joy is full overflowing
in the clear eyes.
you look at mine more calmly.

Now your clear eyes
are bathed in tears; yet,
quiet one, you show a growth
of smile about your mouth.

In this endless tenderness
of the clear well —
talking and thinking,

my swimming flashes
the scales in ecstasies
along the dream of a goldfish.

KIM KYU-DONG (1923–), a journalist and publisher, published two books of poetry, *The Butterfly and Square* (1955) and *Modern Myth* (1958). Also he has published a book of criticism on poetry.

Kim Kyu-dong

ARMY CEMETERY

The army shoes
    thrown away on the road
The shoes and road and mountains
    are bleeding like a landscape
    painted by Salvador Dali

A silence to eternity
    swelling in the cobalt sky
White tomb stones
The laughter of the war dead
    melts away through a far desert
Each poor short life
    speaks to the noises
    in the other world

Waves of a vision as white as cloud —
    the fighters were skimming
    over the smoky jungles those days

A helmet tumbles about
    in an empty wide plain
The cemetery in the afternoon
    is walking to me
    waving the silver papers

KIM CH'A-YŎNG (1924–), a journalist, attended Ritsumeikan University, Kyoto, Japan. He was a member of the Latter-Half Period group, and his poems were anthologized in *The Modern Temperature* (1957).

Kim Ch'a-yŏng

A POETIC FOUL

Tomorrow is rejected. My throat will remain silent.

Today plans to disappear, and in that disappearance I play a poetic foul.

Nothing is left in a city of myself. My sun has set. In my desert, there exists nothing like thirst for salt, melancholy of reason, or imaginary decadency. There is none of mine, nothing like an endless image, a cooled planet, jealousy or love's lie, anxiety in the cloudy memory, or even love which is sustained by the anxiety.

Everything that is to occupy my space will lose its archetype, and my body will be conquered by time.

I throw away the motive of my recollection from the white stairs of my geometrical mind. There is my future right there, and my throat will remain silent.

KIM KWAN-SIK (1924–), a student of Chinese and Korean classics, published two volumes of verse, *Falling Flowers* (1952) and *Selected Poems* (1956). He has also written articles on history and Chinese poetry.

Kim Kwan-sik

DIARY OF CAVERN LIFE

When the sun rises
he crawls out
from the cave
to play outside.

When he is hungry,
a bowl of vegetable soup
and two or three spoonfuls
of rice always suffice.
When sleepy, he just sleeps.

He enjoys the sunlight on his back,
sitting squat,
naked,
with the cleaned rags
spread over the rock.

When the sun sets
he crawls back
into the cave
to pass another night.

PAK YANG-GYUN (1924–), a graduate of Sŏnggyun'gwan University, started publishing poetry in the *Munye* magazine in 1950. He has a book of verse, *A Landmark Left Behind*.

Pak Yang-gyun

WINDOW

The window is inclined
to trust night, and I the window.
In this darkness, no relief will do,
the window enlarges its breadth.
Leaning against it, which longs
for the outflowing emotion,
I am waiting for relief
even though I doubt you.
I cannot help but trust the window,
and the window, night.

SIN TONG-JIP (1924–), a graduate of Seoul University, also studied at Indiana University in 1957, and is presently teaching at Yŏngnam University, Taegu, Korea. He published four books of poetry, *Noonday*, *The Banishment of Lyricism* (1954), *The Second Prelude* (1958), and *Boiling Vowels* (1965). He won the Asia Foundation's Free Literature Prize in 1954.

Sin Tong-jip

LIFE

Has life become soiled?
Half is clay-colored
and the ruined face expressionless.

I was so eager to survive
and thirsted for living with you,
to become one lovelier than death.

Starlight comes and touches
inside my life, after passing darkness
for a hundred million light years.

Still in the memory of cannon's flames
we call the lost names, those names
soaked warmly in our bodies.

The living, testify in favor of the dead.
The dead men, prosecute the living.
The condition of life is solitude.

Looking back, I see afar a long way.
The wind blows in high-spirited sway
behind me far off over there.

Come back, alive, my swan,
to a breathing place which will vanish
into a certain, much longer time.

Sin Tong-jip

POETRY

When the day breaks in town
I see myself lie down
among the locked lines.

— The shells, spread over the morning beach.
The dead white blood-corpuscles night left.
— I crawl out of those characters.

Walking between the stanzas
I have to hold today, which is for me,
which must be shining somewhere.

My feet reach, separate from me,
the front of a large letter
near a closed door.

When I am through with my daily work
and night falls down over the town,
a light comes up in each letter.

Free in the light.
I walk by myself for a while
between the stanzas again.

Then I turn into a narrow lane
in the gap between the broken pieces
of a letter, which refuses to lead me home.

YI PONG-NAE (1924–), a critic, poet, film script writer, and film director, used to write poetry in Japanese while he was staying in Tokyo. After returning to Korea, he wrote modernistic poetry and criticism in Korean as a member of the Latter-Half Period group.

Yi Pong-nae

THE WAR IN THE PAST TENSE

A fountain leaping in the lungs.
It changed into blood and was flowing in
the bowels like a canal of original sin,

when
I sat on the womb
chewing many words
with my yellow teeth like corn.

Our conversation
    was about to end.

Floatings full in the lead-colored sky.
They changed into my dead body and fixed
in time like a specimen of butterfly,

when
I lay down in a show-room
looking at many walls
with my black eyes like female genitals.

Our conversation
    was already over.

YI YONG-SANG (1924–), a graduate of Koryŏ University and formerly a major in the Korean Army, is now working for the South Korean government. He published two books of poetry including *Beautiful Life.*

Yi Yong-sang

I CAN LOVE NORTH KOREANS
To my comrade, Sgt. Richard

Again I see it all noble
like a painting by Millais —
one day in the desolate battle field,
you had found an enemy's body, and
dug a grave while the sun was setting,
and then put a cross before it.

To you who came across the rough ocean
a thousand miles away to a foreign land,
leaving everything lovely far behind,
the enemy must have meant to be
what should be hated and burned up . . .

For all, you said,
" 'I love North Koreans,'
I only hate Communism."
You buried the enemy's body
and prayed before a cross.

When you and the cross stood together
casting shadows in the bright sunset,

no fight between the Free and Communists
was in your peaceful mind;
you were hearing the cathedral bell
ringing out far from your home.
Your prayer for the peace of the world
was beautiful as the early morning star.
" 'I love North Koreans,'
I only hate Communism."

How many times I have muttered
to myself the words you said,
the warm tears trickling down,
thinking of you chanting "Halleluiah."

YI WŎN-SŎP (1924–), a graduate of Hehwa College and a teacher, started publishing poetry in the *Yesul Chosŏn* in 1948, followed by the *Munye* in 1949. His first book of verse, the *Hyangmisa*, came out in 1953, and won the Korean Writers Association Award in 1960. He also translated classic Chinese poetry.

Yi Wŏn-sŏp

PEARL

When I long for the sea, it will do
to take out a shell and look at it.
This one, too,
must be so thirsty.
Let me steep it in water
full in a bowl
so that it may weep
like a serpent in the moonlight,
may cry missing home.
Longing, the cold and hard thing
may, then, conceive a pearl.

HONG YUN-SUK (1925–), pseudonym, Yŏsa, studied at Seoul University and published three books of verse, including *Poems by Yŏsa* (1962) and *On Toillette* (1968). She has recently experimented with a poetic drama.

Hong Yun-suk

ON TOILLETTE

It is coquetry, like nasals
with which women would
call men in the primitive wood,
for a woman to make her toillette
one after another, isn't it?

Shining necklace on the dewy neck,
fluttering earrings down the lobes.
Aren't they flower-nectars
to attract butterflies,
or rouge and powder
of a tempting flower?

(To me, a leaf of grass
shaking in myself like light air
flickering in a looking glass,
— to the other I,
toillette is the autumn sun's
delicate coloration.)

Like a sweet wink, however,
like a smile of a quiet girl,
the renewing color and fragrance
often speak for love in elegance.

So woman spends, once in a while,
the whole hours before a mirror

for the sake of her hidden word.
After all, I am afraid, this is
a miscalculation of the world.

KIM YUN-SŎNG (1925–), a journalist, once said, "the writing of poetry means the finding of a style." He published a book of verse, *The Mountain-path Where the Sea Is Seen* (1959).

Kim Yun-sŏng

BIRD IN THE EARLY MORNING

I hear a sparrow
in the early morning at the window;
quiet and sweet.
While I hear I may forget, and then
suddenly hear again while I forget
the joyful singing.
In the clear air early in the morning
my mind gets all the calmer
for the sweet murmur.
But now, with the midday noise,
my little bird,
where are you gone, no more heard?

KO WON (1925–), given name, Sŏng-wŏn, studied English at Tongguk and London, creative writing at Iowa, and comparative literature at New York University. He has traveled widely, published five volumes of Korean poetry, including *Antinomic Contradiction* (1954) and *At the Time Appointed with Eyes* (1960), and completed a book of English poems.

Ko Won

FACING MIDNIGHT

Only what is left is beautiful, they say,
or what fades, alone is precious.
Whose is that cold footstep, anyway,
which seeks me at this hour
to force me to such a thought?

The windows of night are open, illuminations
at the secret meeting place of death and life.
Another day sits on the edge of the chair
calculating the gain and loss of virtuous fear,
that is the order late at night.

Fear is perhaps
a quality of enduring flesh.
The skull has opened all the doors
facing a moonless midnight with a dog barking.

My hands are grasping
the structure of the countless broken stars,
my eyes watch an island which is not on a map
and a time which is not in history,
and ears alert for the voice of a watcher
hear the foggy silence of the flowing wind.

Lips are closed,
while the leaves fall
at the foot of a wall.

Resisting the weight of silence
which has come through tears,
drop by drop, or streak by streak,
the lamplight grows under my skin
still facing midnight.

Ko Won

THE MEANING OF FLAGS

Black cries of crows
through the black clouds,
out of which the panting flags
were scattering chevrons and decorations.

The sky of "fatherland" in strange utterance
was a colony of flags deported from earth.
In the hardened air, flags seemed to vary
in proportion to the flying crows.
The century suffered from too many flags.

Stars cold,
weapons hot.
Young men, anesthetized with noise,
got used to kill their dreams most exactly.

Bullet-shells of history
on the corpse of meaning. Now, the torn
symbols are haughty, riding on high again.
Have they ever, in fact, loved anyone
enough to tear at themselves like that?

Camouflage with the black wind and wings.
A war was anyhow a uniform or a sign.
Let me say, you banners,
only the sleeves of an insane widow.

Ko Won

A CHEVAL GLASS COVERED

There, a middle-aged pretty woman
sleeping with her dead dog.
She dreamed of a bloody man
smashing the mirror, alone,
trying to cut off his parts in it.

Still naked before the glass,
she felt his blood around her breasts,
crying and turning round all day long
till she tore a coal-black evening dress
and covered the dead dog's large image with it.

When asked what it was all about,
she muttered to herself: what was there
wasn't really he or she, or swan . . .
the looking glass was a rammed time,
and the world ever lay behind the glass.

SONG UK (1925–), a graduate of Seoul University where he teaches English literature, studied at the University of Michigan. He first appeared in the *Munye* magazine, and published two books of poetry, *Temptation* (1954), and *Hayŏ Chi Hyang* (1961).

Song Uk

ROSES

A rose bush.
Around the red petals
the green leaves dense
and the thorns
sharp in the sun.

I will dance
stark-naked.
Stretching my legs
washed by tears
I will dance
till the red sun sets.

A rose bush.
When my blood drops
flowers will drink it.
When I become exhausted
muffling in the leaves
new flowers will bloom
with my flesh on each thorn.

YI CHONG-HAK (1925–) majored in art at Seoul University. He
has published a book of poetry, *Flower Garden* (1955).

Yi Chong-hak

POPULATION

On the wall of bread
    withered mouth
    chimney of black neck
    rusty nails
    sequence of cutting
The heat of sticky soil
    the dead river
    and the war fallen there
    bony frame of a castle
    and tombstones

Toward evening
    a scarecrow laughs
In the back yard of bread
with shaking green
    the wind laughs
In the waving golden field
of corn and in its memories
    a crow laughs

Shall we wait at the end of time

A flag is hoisted
Flowers are working
The withering hands are moving
    last in the bloody field

of increasing labor
Death and population
        implanted in a subway

It is a funny transportation
The wrecked ship on these
broken two seas
In the furrow of some richness
        you may think of beer
        corn brothers
        a sunny harvest over there
        death and
        victory

CHANGHO (1926–), real name, Kim Chang-ho, a graduate of
Tongguk University, published a book of poetry, *Chorus of Reptiles*
(1957), in addition to the trio anthology, *The Railway Station without Timetable* (1952), in collaboration with Yi Min-yŏng and Ko
Won, and some poetic drama. He is now leading the Korea Poetic
Drama Society.

Changho

GASLIGHTS FOR THE STORM

This is the time to light
gaslights for the storm.

Let those who have left be gone.
On the land for more people to live
the coal-black night, like negation,
has not prepared to leave.

What can we see here?
The village shrine's walls biting the shrapnel,
and a heap of the dead with the ribs laid bare,
looking up at the sky, on the good faith of man
who tumbles about in mud.

The play of a Pierrot, trying composedly
to smooth this total darkness with yellow gloves,
should have come to the end already.

This is the time to light
gaslights for the storm.
Budding youth is now
blooming like a hymn.

Even if the raging billows,
not Noah's Flood, overflow all the earth,
the burning, burning light of freedom
shall shine bright.

It shall shine endlessly bright
on the waves of plague
which will go down someday at last.

CH'OE IN-HŬI (1926–58), a graduate of Tongguk, first appeared in the *Munye* in 1905, and since then has published poems in a few magazines. He was a member of the *Ch'ŏngp'odo* group.

Cho'oe In-hŭi

THE SETTING SUN

Full at the ridge, the sunlight looks like rising by itself,
and the blueness of pine trees is quiet all the more.

Too far from friends to be with,
I grope my way up a mountain-path.

Standing mutely, zelkova trees watch time,
and the cloudy fog melts on the rocks, no longer stuck.

And there the covert sound of bell,
shaking the air, comes through.

Beyond a slope, a temple gate is open, antiquated in red and blue,
with a brook down behind, washing the white stones.

Tiles on the roof, a thousand years old,
getting dark, still remain green.

CHŎN YŎNG-GYŎNG (1926–), a graduate of Yŏnse, concentrates on satirical subjects with colloquialisms, often criticizing political and social affairs. He has published three volumes of this kind, the latest one entitled *My Taste Is Solitude*.

Chŏn Yŏng-gyŏng

A SILLY YOUNG MAN WHO ASKS WHAT LIFE IS

Since the eventful twenty years had gone with the flowers, you
    had borne the night-long solitude and friendship; since you
    were fond of Bach's Eternity or Beethoven's Fate, you
    thought of something like the sea and mountains, willy-nilly,
    like the trees, again willy-nilly rocks and animals; during
    another ten years struggling with poverty and anger, you have
    had a sad time because of your weakness and goodness. Like
    an apology after misunderstanding, you have been smoking,
    drinking, half in despair, half from curiosity, and loved a
    toddling stubborn parrot.
And then with heart like the vast Manchurian plain, you slept
    with a recklessly tail-wagging snake; sucking, eating, dis-
    charging, playing, at random. And next, with heart like
    Hamlet which you read when you were at secondary school,
    heart like shortly after 5 p.m., June 25, 1950, with glaring
    eyes and lips firmly closed, with amazingly trembling fists
    and the shabby life, you cleared your throat terribly chilled,
    acted rudely and did wrong with no care at all, and regretting
    everything you were painful and felt awful. Next, next,
    next . . . , in the lawless horrifying world, three years again
    stirring your bile and every season with the teasing children
    passed. Since then your laugh sometimes became a cudgel,
    sometimes a hill, or the national treasury the South Gate in
    Seoul, or a rice bag, or even pork indeed; your loud laugh
    became a nation in various ways like flowers.

And to you, the God damned women — whether a gold-bearing woman, a big woman in her private car, a woman wearing an apron, or a beauty with powdered face — have been the wind, flower, the moon and an elegy; or a woman who asked you to tell about E. A. Poe, or any other kind has been no more than a criminal harbor. And now at the West Gate and at a poor stand-shop, under the many many stars, you spit at last after long patience, turning back, and go to a public latrine in Chongno which is our Havana.

HAN MU-HAK (1926–) studied philosophy at Waseda, Tokyo. He published three books of poetry, including *What You and I Mean* (1964).

Han Mu-hak

A YOUNG MESSENGER WHO WATCHES NIGHT

Say, let us call day like this night.

Night is gone,
but dawn does not return,
and a small dog barks
even at night in such worrying tones.

Only pure darkness will suffice for night.
What is branding an evil iron
still fiercely piercing heart,
and makes you bark at day-in-night
sitting up all night long?

Say, let us call day like this night.

Only quietness will suffice for night.
Who is driving nails noisily
in the top of a poor coffin,
and makes you bark at day-in-night
with ears on end?

Say, let us call day like this night.

Only a sweet breath of air will suffice for night.
What national policy is cremating all
good-natured people with firewood in thick smoke,

and makes you bark at day-in-night
with nose sticking high in the air?

Let us hurry, all of us,
along with that little dog,
let us break down the heavy door —
the door of darkness — to the end
even if we will bleed in dark blue again
from our wounded shoulders and more.

Say, let us call day like this night.

KIM CHONGGIL (1926–), given name, Ch'i-gyu, a graduate of Koryŏ University where he teaches English poetry, also studied at Sheffield University, England. He published a book of poetry, *Christmas* (1968), translations (both English and Korean), and criticisms.

Kim Chonggil

THE EVENING GLOW

The glow, how many times has it come back to swallow
morning and evening, Your time, and then to vanish?
Now the glow touches and soaks into my cheeks.

The glow brings the sound of the evening bell,
a thousand years old, with flowers falling,
in the tile-blue of the Silla dynasty.

As I now wake up from a short dream
which led me into the glow, into eternity,
the blue East Sea setting far away
fills up my vision, the entire body.

KU CHA-UN (1926–), who studied at Sŏnggyun'gwan University, is interested in fine art, and his poetic sense often combines with artistic vision.

Ku Cha-un

CRACKS

Cracks
on a finely polished stone face.
Some are sore and tangled, making a wedge;
others, faintly flowing, form a nude woman.
And others, slowly rolling down, hang about
the lower part of the woman, like the leaves.

They let me meditate for a while:
the frailty of these cracks
(yes, it might be accidental)
will sound crisp in my gaunt bones
when I grow old, and sometimes
charm me in fickle dreams.

PAK IN-HWAN (1926–56) was a student of medicine and later a journalist. He appeared in an anthology, *A New City and the Citizens' Chorus* (1949), and his *Selected Poems* came out in 1955, shortly before his death.

Pak In-hwan

THE LAST CONVERSATION

The shadow of a city escapes
without noise.
Vision flows endlessly
under the shades of turning age
and innumerable impressions.
Such a tangle of anxiety
as the inclined newspapers.

The carnival of bars at random.
Negro's trumpet.
Scream of a European bride.
Emperor of spirit.
Who knows my secret?
I experience more
on this phantom bed
in a quiet room.

Origin of reminiscence.
City of full disgrace.
Sunset exile.
Something I hear when I bend
my neck into the black overcoat.

O that hoarse requiem,
I hate it forever.
Shall we be able to meet again

in the ruins of today?
We, the mission of nineteen fifty.

Chrysanthemums have bloomed
against the background of the sick sea.
The gardens of the closed universities
are now cemeteries.
Coming behind paintings and reason,
the last uneasy conversation
surges like waves
holding the arms of the drunken mariners.

Pak In-hwan

BLACK GOD

Who is it that cries in the graves over there
Who is it that comes out of the broken buildings
What was it that faded like smoke in the dark sea
What begins after a year's ending
Where can I see the friend war took away
  Give me death instead of sorrow
  Cover the world with blizzard
   in place of men
   so that no flower may bloom
   where the buildings and pale tombs were

Miserable memory of a day a year and the war
It must be your favorite subject
  black God

KIM NAM-JO (1927–) majored in Korean literature at Seoul University and is presently teaching at Sukmyŏng Women's University. She has published four volumes of poetry, *Life* (1952), *The Perfumed Oil of Nard* (1955), *The Tree and the Wind* (1958), and *The Flag of Mind* (1959). The later poems are more inclined to Catholicism. She won the Korea Free Literature Association Prize in 1958.

Kim Nam-jo

MY BABY HAS NO NAME YET

My baby has no name yet;
like a new-born chick or a puppy,
my baby is not named yet.

What numberless texts I examined
at dawn and night and evening over again!
But not one character did I find,
which is as lovely as the child.

Starry field of the sky,
or heap of pearls in the depth.
Where can the name be found, how can I?

My baby has no name yet;
like an unnamed bluebird or white flowers
from the farthest land for the first,
I have no name for this baby of ours.

Kim Nam-jo

FLAG OF MIND

My mind is a flag.
It has been flying as if it does not exist
in time and space that no one sees.

Unable to bear its own
confusion and fever,
it has come out to a snowy crossroads.

Like smoke, an easy shade
spreads on the snow.
The flag of my mind may now be
listening to the snow music.

It wants nothing but
the unregretted sunset
piled silently like petals.

Is there no friend with such nature
as the white sands, where a deep grief
like an imperial surrender has sunken clean?

My mind
is a flag.

Sometimes it cries
and sometimes prays
in time and space that no one sees.

KIM YO-SŎP (1927–), a graduate of Chŏngjin Teachers College
and a journalist, is presently secretary of the Korean Poets Associa-
tion. He writes both poetry and juvenile literature, and has published
two books of poetry, *Weight* and *The Moon and Machine.*

Kim Yo-sŏp

SHOOTING AT THE MOON

Every night in the town,
a boy was shooting arrows at the darkness.

His arrows flew to hit the white stars.
In the town where the meteors fell and the boy slept,
a nightmare was lit up like a lamp every night.

Once an arrow
hit the heart of the moon.

The moon shed her white blood in a stream.
The moonlight drenched the earth and the boy's dream.

The boy died with the moonlight tied round his neck.
He died in the park holding a bow in his hand.

The white moon which has lost her songs
is now lit up alone over the fountain.

MUN TŎK-SU (1927–) graduated from Hongik College, where he is presently teaching. He published a book of poetry, *Ecstasy*, in 1956. He also edits a poetry magazine.

Mun Tŏk-su

AN INTERNAL IMAGE

A stone rolls down the long
dark green spiral stairs.
That is the fossil of a bird
my sister freed one night.
The doves over the City Hall
sit on the white scruff of her neck,
while a fist-size stone rolls down.
Worn and sharpened, rubbing itself
like her hard struggle, the stone
becomes God's staff and stands up.
It goes down unsteadily walking.
There is a branch in the cold spring
as big as a rib of the dead widow.
The stone staff, now like the branch,
steps down the stairs as if dancing.
The stone, born of a dream of the wind
which was flying up covering the earth
with thousands of its flapping skirts
shaking this branch, groping about
the Mediterranean in my sister's eyes.
A stone rolls down the long
dark green spiral stairs.

NO MUN-CH'ŎN (1927–), a high school teacher, graduated from Usŏk University and has published a book of verse, *Mummy*. Also he edited an anthology of modern love poems.

No Mun-ch'ŏn

MYŎNG DONG, SEOUL

The thirsty sea along the flickering neons.
From the hill of anguish
I throw a stone, which brings no ripple.

The thick mist of gipsyish nostalgia
over the blue harbor of the running century.
The noise leads the expressionless blindness.

As the sun sets, it gets lighter.
On every pagan street, the thirst of all becomes
the angry waves swallowing innocence.

Canoeing with laughter at the back
people wander about — my lovely jungle.

Shall we pick up the floating flowers
from the crazy billows before the bloody hands
invite devils with cruel cry in the shocking light,
and exchange the bitter, old stories?

CHŎN PONG-GŎN (1928–) is, in his words, "interested in writing chanson." His poems were collected in *Repetition for Love* (1959) besides in a three-man anthology, *The War and Music and Hope* (1957), and he received the Korean Poets Association Award. He also published a collection of essays, *In Search of Poetry* (1961), and a long poem, *The Love Song of Ch'unhyang* (1967).

Chŏn Pong-gŏn

BARBED WIRE

Darkness, a snowy field, and the barometer falling.

The loudspeaker, which started clear broadcast at the point where the marching flute had stopped thirteen hours before, carries the sound of a woman's voice again.

I think for a while of the fact that I did not know how to begin to cross myself and of the face of an army chaplain with a loud voice.

"Break."

This is a squad of feelers, as delicate and tough as those of a butterfly, that sense the boughs, stones, ice, dangerous ice field, and the water and rocks under them.

A sudden attack.
A night advance deploying like a ballet.
Continuity of sound-waves, more and more minute.

I think that I must keep myself within forty yards of the loudspeaker for the blue flash of the signal bullet to be accurate.

Every morning I hear the sound of somebody drawing water not far away and the sound of wings, dove wings.

I am conscious of the barbed wire around me.

Chŏn Pong-gŏn

FLOWER IN A CLASSIC WHISPER

Everywhere
your hands
meet mine.
If you
want it
so eagerly,
I will become
a forsaken moss
or a stone
wherever,
for a thousand years.
Yes,
when your hands
touch me, oh then
a thousand years become one moment.
You are
within my grasp
already.
Between the field furrows in Kyŏngju,
you become a huge lightning flash
which burns up darkness;
become an immortal element of the sky's blue;
an ever-flowing rich river,
holding and embracing countless deaths;
something hot that runs over your eyes,
dewdrops engraved with ten, a hundred, a thousand suns, and
    yourself falling down to your all souls and bodies, waiting
    for such as you.
Have you seen endless youth?
At such a time, you are a leaf on a root, a fruit on a leaf,
and a root on a fruit.
Presently you become the sweet sound of a flute
lasting a thousand years —
it is because
I am this joy of yours,

of human being,
and of brilliant life.
Someone's fingerprint that, a thousand years ago,
killed darkness and killed death.
I also am that fingerprint,
marked on a stone.

Chŏn Pong-gŏn

HOPE

The reason why I think of a beautiful
a certain beautiful day ahead

why I want to be a flower
and an apple in a flower-basket
around your mouth

why I think
of dew clean in the moonlight
the dawn breaking while the pearly
dewdrops form on the cabbages
dove's eyes moist with the sea
the sky coming down with a smile
azaleas on the blue stairs
and the street-trees through which
the newspapers have flowed like music

here
at night with snow
piled among the trees
bearing many bullet-wounds
here where the trees lost their songs
that faded away from each wound

the reason why
thinking of two willow necklaces
I want to be a flower
and an apple in a flower-basket
around your mouth

is that
I the self

longing for cloud
the earth
and man
stand dreamily
like haze
on my eyelids from where
the war has scattered

KIM KWANG-NIM (1928–), a magazine editor, seeks for "intellectual lyricism" in poetry. He has published three books, *Sorrowful Grafting* (1959), *Image's Light Shadow* (1962), and *Morning's Cast-net* (1965).

Kim Kwang-nim

GOLDFISH

Do the seeds scattered
by the blazing evening sun
wriggle about in a glass bowl?

The goldfishes
light the lamp-wick
a poor man cleaned.

They never show
themselves off,
nor care for
their own brightness.

The goldfishes
flaming up
in haze
on which the dewy
sunlight blooms.

SIN TONG-MUN (1928–), a journalist and member of the Post-war Writers Association, attended Seoul University. He won the annual literary contest of the *Chosŏn Ilbo* in 1956, and published a book of poetry, *A Balloon and the Third Creeping* (1956). He was the winner of the first Ch'ungbuk Literary Award.

Sin Tong-mun

AGE

One day in the field I saw something like a broken
  piece of celadon china flash in the evening sun.

The other day I saw something like a woman's hair
  thrown away beside a garbage can.

Yesterday I laughed at myself for imitating a loud
  weeping by chance on my way to somewhere.

This morning, looking at blood on the toothbrush,
  I was fancying myself an old bachelor.

I think tomorrow I will visit a dejected friend of
  mine whom I haven't seen for a long time.

YI KYŎNG-NAM (1929–), a journalist, attended Pyongyang Teacher's College before coming to the South during the Korean War. His poems gained recognition in the *Hyŏndae Munhak* in 1956–57.

Yi Kyŏng-nam

CONSTITUTION

A little grade-schoolboy, the son of my friend, had come with an old book of the constitution and asked me what it was; I could give him no answer, and instead gazed at him vacantly.

And then a college student, so he claims, who lives next door to me, came with a new book of the constitution and seemed ready to talk endlessly about the law one page after another along with what was going on in the world; I offered him a cup of tea trying to get him to leave me.

Both of them looked displeased and cheeky when they left. Sending them off at the gate, I, looking likewise, was surprised to feel the raindrops on my brow, and looked up at the sky where the starlight, like my mother's navel cord, which had seemed in the same way to be delighted at looking down at me, was now laughing in an unusual manner. It looked as though roaring with laughter, as if holding its aching navel.

SŎNG CH'AN-GYŎNG (1930–) majored in English at Seoul University, and first appeared in the *Munhak Yesul* in 1956. His book of verse is *The Stake Counterpart.*

Sŏng Ch'an-gyŏng

THE SONG OF A FIREFLY

Wind blows. Christ
roams about forever.
The sun rises, round
like Goethe's book.
A rainbow appears.
Valéry's adding-machine.
A brook —
the Eastern sages
flow on.
At night
I also scatter
a dim light
around there, whereas
the stars are bright.
I realize
Spinoza replaced
a hundred thousand eyes.

HWANG UN-HŎN (1931–) is a graduate of Yŏnse with a major in English. A journalist, he first appeared in the *Munhak Yesul* in 1957. He is a member of the *Hyŏndaesi* group.

Hwang Un-hŏn

A WILD SHOT

Absolute gray
over the window.
The sea seemed to move about
in the stove where winter had sunk.
A cold-looking little boy
shot the bird with a hunting gun.
While the downy wings are strewn
at the end of a dead tree,
the moon hangs in deep blue
a death by hanging.

PAK HŬI-JIN (1931–), member of the Post-war Writers Association, majored in English at Koryŏ University, and published a book of poetry, *Chamber Music*, in addition to his translation of *Gitanjali* by Tagore.

Pak Hŭi-jin

MAGICIAN

He bites a lamp bulb and swallows it;
receives seething lead with tongue
and cools it in his mouth; stands
barefoot on a sharpened scythe;
pierces his throat with a long skewer
and hangs buckets, full of water,
on both ends. No single drop
of water or blood he sheds. Yo-ho!
A magician, one who earns money
risking his neck. A magician, bravo!

I, too, am a magician in dream.
It's nothing for me to tumble about
stark-naked in a thorn thicket. Swallow
stars, make them roses at the finger ends;
draw the heart out through the ribs; walk
about standing on my head with a brain
on the soles of my feet. No single drop
of blood or sweat I shed. Yo-ho!
A magician, one who dreams
risking his neck. A magician, bravo!

PAK SŎNG-NYONG (1931–), a journalist and member of the
Post-war Writers Association, attended Chungang University. His
poetry first appeared in the *Munhak Yesul* magazine in 1956.

Pak Sŏng-nyong

A WINDY DAY

Does it mean
for the wind
to be restless specially today
that the wind knows, as well as I do,
I am losing everything I have?

Does it mean
that the wind knows, as well as I do,
I am also losing everything I have
like the autumn leaves being swept
cleanly on the grass
on the branches
in the field and village?

O, does it mean for the wind
to feel that uneasy now
that the wind knows, as well as I do,
today I am aware of all
I don't have, too?

YI CH'ANG-DAE (1931–) majored in history at the Graduate School of Tongguk University. He first appeared in the *Munhak Yesul* in 1957, and published his first book of poetry, *Horrible Play*, in 1966.

Yi Ch'ang-dae

ELEGY

Though the emptiness grieves me,
on your leaving,
I will never say what parting is.
Though the wind comes to me
with sad sobs,
though the bell ringing there
sounds so lonely,
I will listen calmly to them,
accepting pleasure from the pain.
Though my heart is restless by the river,
I will never say what parting means.
While you have left
and the emptiness hurts me,
please let your shadow
sleep in my body.

YI HYŎNG-GI (1931–), a journalist, majored in Buddhism at Tongguk, and has published poems and criticism since 1949, when his poetry appeared in the *Munye* monthly. He was awarded the Korean Writers Association Prize in 1957.

Yi Hyŏng-gi

THE LAST STREETCAR

Far away, creaking,
goes the last streetcar
laden with last expectation.

Vivid wheels in my heart.
A woman,
will you shed tears there?

In a bedroom of the weak
the moon will shine, tonight,
the merciful bright moon.

It is warm — the moonlight,
who passes her hand
over the hands stained with life.

Joy and sorrow, let's say,
are merely light hail, or such
an indifferent grace.

Outside the window where I pillow
my head on my arm, no matter where,
goes the last streetcar.

MIN CHAE-SIK (1932–), a graduate of Koryŏ University with a major in English, first published his poetry in the *Munhak Yesul* magazine in 1956. His book is *Sheep of Atonement*.

Min Chae-sik

FRIDAY
— eli eli lama sabakdani?

1

It rains every Friday.
When Friday comes the rain comes
along the road where smog falls.

Dim faces on a train's steamed windows.
Celluloid in an X-ray.
A way as if only for going,
a never returning way.

2

The road burns.
It burns in the headlights.
A long corridor in a ward burns.

Each streak of the rain catches fire,
and arrows run into the sky.

A thing left behind burns.
A thing being carried out also burns.
The eyes stained with fire burn too.

The road, wet in the rain.
The wet and burning road.
On Friday, it rains at night too.

SIN KI-SŎN (1932–) attended Tongguk University and won recommendation in the *Munhak Yesul* magazine in 1956. He is a member of the Poetic Drama Society and of the Cine-poem Society.

Sin Ki-sŏn

FLESH

It must be a warehouse.
Made of the moonlight, cut to fit,
full of the manufactured goods, depressing,
it must be a warehouse.

With the door opening in the morning sun
and closing in the sunset,
tons of words sleeping here,
it must be a warehouse.

Hanging time, a thousand,
a hundred million years' time,
all dried up,
on the wall in full,
it must be a warehouse.

One, do, three, fall —
mathematics, calculation of joy and sadness,
clustering like the sprouting leaves,
it must be a cruel warehouse.

And yet, incapable
of looking at itself forever,
the agonizing gum collecting in the eye,
it must be a wretched,
wretched warehouse.

SIN TONG-YŎP (1932–69), a graduate of Tan'guk College and a teacher, won a poetry prize in the *Chosŏn Ilbo* literary contests in 1959. He published a long poem *Asanyŏ* and poetic drama.

Sin Tong-yŏp

NO

No,
I have never hated.
On the crest of a mountain
with the clear sunlight pouring forth,
how could I conceive of anger?

No,
I have never been in agony.
Beyond the ridge
where the silken music flows,
who could shed tears, too beautiful to show?

No,
I have never loved.
While I am happy with the air
alone on the world's roof,
how could I love any clothed town's girl?

CH'OE SŎL-LYŎNG (1933–) published her first book of poetry, *About the Time When I Put Out the Lamp*, in 1964. She received an M.A. in Korean from Ewha and an M.S. in Education from St. John's University, New York.

Ch'oe Sŏl-lyŏng

ELEGY

So pale Julian, against the wall.
An emptiness, a ghost with feet
over his sense-lost shoulders.

The painless parting
withdraws near the hill,
and the deaf night sits at table.

In myself, dissolving
like the slowly disappearing mist,
the locked-in remorse lingers.

The anger of yesterday that was
rushing to an extreme has gone,
leaving a heavy, grey being behind.

Life, the dead leaf, falls
down the dull parallel lines.
Is the moon a death-engraving juggler?

The night river of craving
flows as a rose blooms
on an old battle field.

The broken possibilities, buried
in a place to return to, after all.
A prototype falls asleep by Julian.

KO ŬN (1933–), student of Buddhism, has recently given up his career as a professional Buddhist. He published his first book of poetry, *The Nirvana Sensibility* (1960).

Ko Ŭn

AUTUMN SONG

Speech is a poor thing.
The moonlit earth is an artist,
it is real.
I have spoken enough
with eyes that could see nothing.
I have spoken much, enough, about
existence, nothingness, and supplication.
Has Buddha ever listened to me, I wonder,
with his eyes half closed?
And autumn, how can it force me
to say more, about what? How can it
take my soul to a lonely belief?
I have spoken enough. Let me close eyes
that look blankly at the bare branches.
Is Buddha there, again his eyes
half open, to order me to talk?
Oh myself is falsehood, and the earth
is an artist.

PAK CHAE-SAM (1933–) was born in Tokyo and studied at Koryŏ University, Seoul. His poetry first appeared in the *Hyŏndae Munhak*, a literary monthly, in 1955, and won the magazine's award. His publications include a book of verse, *Ch'unhyang's Mind* (1962).

Pak Chae-sam

A CICADA SINGS
from "Ch'unhyang's Mind"

In the broad daylight brightening our mind
    a cicada is singing in the back wood.

A cicada sings with various voices, which in my far
    back childhood used to become flowers or leaves
    or my neighboring good friend's face, all as I
    wished looking up at the clouds,

    and through which today I can hear delightedly
    my lover's beautiful voice, his dependable steps,
    or even the sound of his untying ankle bands.

A cicada sings merrily, merrily.

CHŎNG KONG-CH'AE (1934–), a graduate of Yŏnse University and a journalist, first published poetry in the *Hyŏndae Munhak* in 1958, from which he won the New Writer Prize in 1959. He also has published a few long poems.

Chŏng Kong-ch'ae

COAL

It happened to be piled up by the seaside,
    like us, like life.
The wharf, forming a graveyard
    of the black tombs.

The wind, the black wind passes over,
and the water whispers beneath
like a bad companion,
the black water tempting in low tones.

Piled up by the seaside, by chance,
    like us, like life.

KIM HU-RAN (1934–) studied at Seoul University. She published
a book of verse, *Ornate Knife and Rose.*

Kim Hu-ran

ROSES

An ornate silver knife
held in a woman's hand
fluttering;
at sleeve's length
roses open
to love's tune.

Delicate skirt lines,
lips moist with fruit juice.

The sun smiles with eyes
drunken with fragrance.
The afternoon sun
pierced with rose thorns
bursts into full smile.

PAK PONG-U (1934–) majored in political science at Chŏnnam University. He won the annual literary contest of the *Chosŏn Ilbo*, a daily newspaper, in 1956, and since has published two books of verse, *The Truce-Line* (1957) and *The Trees Flowering Even in Winter* (1959).

Pak Pong-u

KOREAN DOOR-PAPER

I wish I could illustrate tears
— the text vast as the sky —
on Korean door-paper.

A night vast as the sky
which I want to give you
without bringing tears . . . .

I wish I could draw such tears
on Korean door-paper.

SONG HYŎK (1934–) graduated from Tongguk University, where he is now editing the *Tongdae Sinmun* and *The Dongguk Post*. He has published poetry since 1957.

Song Hyŏk

EXPAND YOUR WINGS

The bird with its raucous song,
the caged bird
crying for summer's day
crying for time gone by
over the ever green wood.

The cage like the lonely depths empty of all
forces the bird to call out against dread leisure.

The bird, beating morn and night,
cries out to the sky in smarting soliloquy
running life's course,
and holding pious faith
in the drop of water it pecks up.

Yesterday and today,
what tells the bird to hold back
its cries against the painful barrier
like a closed front door?
Flying the bird,
flying the skies, only in its cage.

Neglecting its own wings,
has the bird need of anyone
at whom should it shoot arrows?
The caged bird
ever flying away.

HWANG MYŎNG-GŎL (1935–) studied French at Seoul University; his poetry was first published in the *Chayu Munhak* in 1962.

Hwang Myŏng-gŏl

THE DEATH OF AN ORPHAN

Mother —
put your hand on my brow for a while, will you?
I have a heavy fever now.
And you say you have no hands.
Is that so? You are right:
I am not your child after all.

Mother —
give me a drop of your milk, will you?
My lips are dried up and burning now.
And you say you have no milk.
Is that so? You are right:
I am not your child after all.

Mother —
hold me at your bosom gently, will you?
I am frozen now.
And you say you have no breasts.
Is that so? You are right:
I am not your child after all.

Mother —
give me a sweet kiss, will you?
I am sleepy now.
And you say you have no lips.
Is that so? You are right:
I am not your child after all.

Jingle bell —
The neon sign of the all-night dancing cabaret
flickers like a boat's light in the river.
The dead body of an orphan is covered with a straw mat
on the icy pavement in front of the Midop'a store,
the torn wrapping papers swept by the sharp wind.

KIM YŎNG-T'AE (1936–), a graduate of Hongik College as an art major, first published in the *Sasanggye* monthly. His book of poetry is *Winter in a Jewish Village* (1965).

Kim Yŏng-t'ae

ON BIRTHDAY
from "Paintings by Chagall"

Winter goes mad
The crazed sky
and the final scream
A bloody hand
enters the room
like Christ
I loose my senses
The morning stars in the straw
melt the frozen blood
of a Jewish woman who has stiffened
into stone
The sound of bells from the village
shrinks with gold the violin strings
of a sleep-walker
A Russian donkey
the groaning clock
the dying clouds
flow away
Blood that congealed in a juniper
becomes a censer to light the wick
of the intestines shaved like a pencil
The first snow falls in the polar regions
for the winter horses that left the ice-field
making the ears of a golden calf
that was attending the church service
open like a morning-glory
while a naked Jewish woman
pours from her navel

a cluster of colors
lumped hard
At the end of the world
the sun
shamefaced
boils water

KIM CHI-HYANG (1937–) has published four volumes of verse including *Sick-room* (1956) and *Black Evening Dress* (1965). She graduated from Hongik College.

Kim Chi-hyang

A DROP OF WATER

A drop of water pecks at my palm.
An illustration moves round.

A bunch of the sunny flowers
rises in the lake.
A blast of shaking breeze
gives birth to a leaf,
and a smiling dimple
crouches down there.

Look,
all directions bear
the mourning badges
as if having been suddenly
drowned in black ink,
crowned with a blueness.

I was drenched in the rain
all the way last night.
Now the rainfall smashes in
to smart my heart.

A drop of water on my palm.
I rub it trying to love
the steps of cold death.

HWANG TONG-GYU (1938–) majored in English at Seoul University and in its Graduate School. He published three volumes of poetry, including *A Certain Clear Day* (1961) and *Elegy* (1965). He also studied at Edinburgh University, and is now teaching at Seoul.

Hwang Tong-gyu

MOONNIGHT

If someone comes and calls me
I will show him the moonlight
falling down on the frozen field,
and an image walking on it.
Of what have I been thinking?
To my friends, some of them,
I will now show the way
which is least lonely to me.
What is left of the pants I so long cared about?
When I step on the ice, both hands raised,
marching the field under the sky suddenly it cleared,
and moonlight fully lights my rags.

MA CHONG-GI (1939–), born in Tokyo, is a graduate of the
Medical College of Yŏnse and also studied at the Graduate School,
Seoul University. He published two volumes of poetry, *Quiet Triumphal Return* (1961) and *The Second Winter* (1965). He is now
studying in the United States.

Ma Chong-gi

A MENTAL HOSPITAL WARD

A mental hospital ward
on the rainy autumn afternoon.

> It is spring, isn't it? Winter comes after spring,
> and then follows a thief. How old am I? Five
> hundred and two. I have exactly twenty-one wives.

This strong young man got sick of preparing
for the civil service examination.
The dead trees are laughing.

> Listen, how can the question be Wagner's style?
> I can do nothing with it but laugh.
> Am I not right? What do you think?

Antique moss grows
at every corner of the ward.

The cries of all kinds of feeling
and the resentment of expectation
splatter the stained wall.

The surface of Narcissus
glitters in the rain.

— Everybody has returned to the proper place.

Here is a student of art, so immersed in the abstract
that she herself has become an abstraction.

It isn't at all boring to look down
at white paper all day long. Say it is fun.

A pierrot, who wore the gown,
weeps only before the rain.

— All have now awoken.

Index of Authors